Quarto.com

First Published in 2025 by Motorbooks, an imprint of The Quarto Group,
100 Cummings Center, Suite 265-D, Beverly, MA 01915, USA.
T (978) 282-9590 F (978) 283-2742

29 28 27 26 25 1 2 3 4 5

ISBN: 978-0-7603-9173-0

Digital edition published in 2025
eISBN: 978-0-7603-9174-7

Library of Congress Cataloging-in-Publication Data

Names: Egan, Sean, author.
Title: Bruce Springsteen and Born to run : 50 years / Sean Egan.
Description: Beverly, MA : Motorbooks, an imprint of The Quarto Group, 2025. | Series: The great albums | Includes index. | Summary: "Bruce Springsteen and Born to Run: Fifty Years is the definitive story of one of the most enduring, appealing, and groundbreaking rock and roll records of all time"— Provided by publisher.
Identifiers: LCCN 2025002557 | ISBN 9780760391730 | ISBN 9780760391747 (ebook)
Subjects: LCSH: Springsteen, Bruce. Born to run. | Rock music—1971-1980—History and criticism.
Classification: LCC ML420.S77 E33 2025 | DDC 782.42166092—dc23/eng/20250122
LC record available at https://lccn.loc.gov/2025002557

Design: Landers Miller Design
Book Cover Image: Bruce Springsteen performs with rhe E Street Band at Alex Cooley's Electric Ballroom in Atlanta, Georgia, on August 22, 1975. *Tom Hill/Getty Images*

Printed in China

BRUCE SPRINGSTEEN & BORN TO RUN 50 YEARS

SEAN EGAN

INTRODUCTION

After more than three decades of towering musical contributions to rock 'n' roll, on November 22, 2016, in Washington, D.C., Springsteen accepted a handshake, hug, and Presidential Medal of Freedom from President Barack Obama. "I am the president, but he is the Boss," Obama said, remarking that Springsteen was "[s]prung from a cage out on Highway 9 . . . a quiet kid from Jersey, just trying to make sense of the temples of dreams and mystery that dotted his hometown."

"He is an American treasure."

That is what President Barack Obama said about Bruce Springsteen in November 2012. Few would argue with the idea that New Jersey native Springsteen is not just a platinum-shifting, stadium-filling rock star but also something far more nuanced and noble. He may be nicknamed "the Boss," but he is a man of the people, making music attuned to the trials and pleasures of the working class. Springsteen has created a glamorous and galvanizing body of work that refracts, reflects, and celebrates unglamorous and unexciting lives. Springsteen's gift is born of the fact that as an individual steeped in post-Elvis popular music—one of the last true believers in rock 'n' roll—he has a profound knowledge of rock alchemy. Nowhere is that knowledge put to greater use than on *Born to Run*, his 1975 breakthrough album that synthesized and refreshed everything good about a medium that many were positing as, after the then-remarkable-seeming lifespan of two decades, outdated at best and approaching obsolescence at worst.

Yet although the album was a massive bestseller and is by common consensus a cast-iron classic, it easily could have never been made. After his first two long players had resoundingly flopped, Springsteen's record label (Columbia) was dubious about him making a third and insisted that he go through the quasi-humiliating process of what amounted to passing a new audition by recording a single first.

Springsteen responded with "Born to Run," a soaring losers' anthem that, once heard, was never forgotten. By doing so, however, he ran himself into a corner, for he could hardly throw the masterpiece that is "Born to Run" onto an LP with a clutch of other tracks that weren't as polished and biting, not least because his third long player might be his last shot at the big time. Springsteen poured fourteen agonizing months

(Above) Bruce Springsteen, age seventeen, in his high school yearbook photo from Freehold High. He may not look very rock 'n' roll at this point, but he already was learning the ins and outs of the stage with his first band, the Castiles.

(Left) The spirit of Elvis Presley seems to inform this promotional photo of Springsteen. Elvis's early TV appearances scandalized a nation accustomed to seeing more demure musical performances. Springsteen caught him on the tube when he was nine and was demanding a guitar the very next day.

of effort into the *Born to Run* album, a tumultuous period during which he lost and replaced band members, gained a new coproducer, switched studios, and drove himself to the brink of a nervous breakdown. The upshot was a triumphant overhaul of his likable but unremarkable formula: His street tableaux and working-class humanitarianism were now given a mythic bent, a high gloss, and a towering scale. As well as the imperishable title track, Springsteen treated listeners to the importunate but elegant ballad "Thunder Road"; the syncopated, brass-punctuated inner-city tableau "Tenth Avenue Freeze-Out"; the day-job decrying "Night"; the anguished poverty reminiscence "Backstreets"; the pulsing pledge of romantic devotion "She's the One"; the downbeat vignette of small-time criminality "Meeting Across the River"; and the climactic youth-culture extravaganza "Jungleland." Despite the epic soundscapes and grand mythologizing, *Born to Run* is also highly gritty by simple virtue of the fact that it explores the nuances of existence of a swath of society normally denied the assumption that it matters.

The cherry on the cake of the critical and commercial success of *Born to Run* was when this long-haired guitarist from short-shrift New Jersey made the cover of *Time* and *Newsweek* on the same day. Two culturally cautious American news magazines simultaneously making a *rock musician* their respective editions' main selling point was a significant acknowledgment of both changing times and Springsteen's own ascendency.

(Left) Springsteen's disheveled appearance at London's Hammersmith Odeon in November 1975 could be said to reflect his perception of his performance, which took place in the depressed aftermath of a controversy about hype. He only revisited the gig decades later, after which he concluded that he had probably overreacted.

With a newly enthusiastic record company behind him, Springsteen and his celebrated E Street Band took the album on the road. While their hyperenergetic and theatrical stage show generated huge enthusiasm and sales large enough to send the record into the top 10, the Springsteen camp also had to fend off criticism about hype, a debate that reached its crescendo when the show moved overseas to the United Kingdom. There, Springsteen not only had to deal with the skeptical British weekly music press but was driven to an infuriated state by the excessive promotional tactics of his label, resulting in him performing his first show at London's Hammersmith Odeon in a fog of despair. Nevertheless, the British audiences—as they have ever since—loved him. Five decades removed, the issue of hype has become an irrelevance: The inhabitants of the States, the UK, and the wider world have long concluded that people love *Born to Run* not because ads or reviews or peer pressure compelled them to but because it was an extraordinary milestone that genuinely moved and excited the public like few other albums.

Bruce Springsteen and Born to Run tells the twisting, turning, tumultuous story of an album that will be cherished as long as radios play, records spin, downloads download, wheels turn, and dreamers dream.

1

GROWIN' UP: THE CONTEXT

Bruce Springsteen's music is often big—gargantuan, even—and never more so than on *Born to Run*. This propensity for grandeur stems from the fact that Springsteen's early years were characterized by a crushing, humiliating sense of smallness—smallness in the sense of coming from a town whose modesty and obscurity offended a man with an innate sense of drama and hankering for glamour; smallness in the sense that he was rarely given cause to believe that he amounted to anything or ever would.

Freehold is a New Jersey town whose population probably never topped ten thousand during the childhood and teen years of Bruce Frederick Joseph Springsteen. It suffered all the drawbacks associated with small towns, but for Springsteen its dead-end nature was exacerbated by it lying adjacent to a far more famous state. Freehold is only a fifteen-minute drive from the buzz and vitality of New York City, but for the young Springsteen it might as well have been a million miles away. "When I was sixteen, man, I hated that town," he told an audience in 1985. "It seemed so narrow-minded and small-minded. I used to get on the bus, take Lincoln Transit to New York City. It used to feel so great when I got out at Port Authority."

While Nowheresville formed the dreary backdrop to Springsteen's formative years, which began on September 23, 1949, there were less abstract and more distressing issues in his daily life. One was poverty—Springsteen had two younger siblings, Virginia (born 1951) and Pamela (born 1962). His father, Douglas, labored through more jobs than anyone could remember but that shared one common and irrefutable fact—they never brought in much money. The same was true of his mother Adele's employment as a secretary. One schoolmate later told writer Christopher Sandford that Springsteen was "dirt-poor."

Springsteen always saw himself as a small-town boy fighting for a meaningful life; for him, if music couldn't provide it, nothing could.

First the Castiles, then Earth, then Steel Mill. In Steel Mill, Springsteen made a name for himself around the Jersey club scene and forged bonds with keyboardist Danny Federici and later Steven Van Zandt. Steel Mill found a groove and a market, opening for the esteemed likes of Grand Funk Railroad, Ike and Tina Turner, and Black Sabbath as well as pulling in crowds of up to four thousand on the strength of their own name.

Springsteen was never comfortable around his father, Douglas, who viewed himself as an abject failure. To make up for this, his dad ran an authoritarian household—something that Springsteen was apt to speak about onstage between songs.

On top of that was the fact that Springsteen spent much of his childhood trying to dodge the invariably disapproving attention of his old man. Douglas was an embittered failure and an authoritarian father who was already exhibiting signs of the mental illness that would come to the fore later in his life. All his son knew then, however, was that his father made him feel uncomfortable every time they were in the same room together, and probably deliberately. His dad would become a big feature of the autobiographical soliloquies that have since early on been a fundamental part of Springsteen's stage act.

A final component of Springsteen's unhappiness was his Catholic schooling in an era when it involved interminable moralizing, endless petty rules, and brutal corporal punishment.

Yet it's difficult to infer that Springsteen's childhood was sheer misery. Most everybody who has ever worked or socialized with him testifies to Springsteen's generosity, patience, compassion, unpretentiousness, and disinclination to bad-mouth or gossip. Someone can only possess such attributes if they have received a lot of love. His saintly mom and to an extent his affectionate maternal grandparents clearly can take the credit here.

Not the least of Springsteen's mother's contributions to his life was her acquiescence to his wish for an electric guitar at the age of fifteen. It was a moment Springsteen in truth had been leading to since he was nine years old when he first saw Elvis Presley

Some of Springsteen's formative years were spent in this modest house in Freehold, New Jersey, a town of less than ten thousand people.

CAFE WHA?
CAFE WHA?
PARKING
ANY
TIME
FREE ADMISSION
ROCK
LIVE!

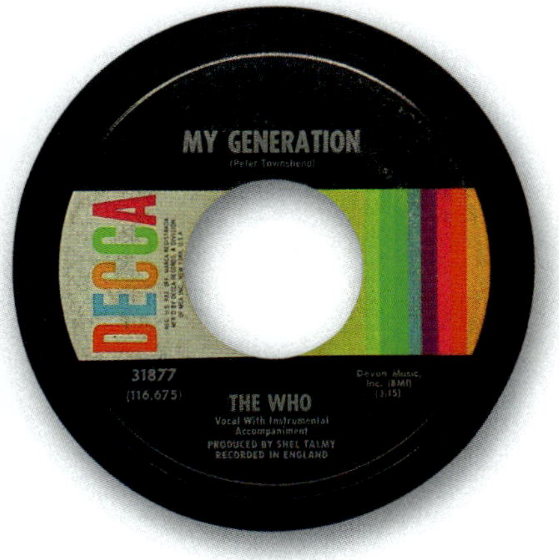

(Above) The Castiles were not opposed to the reverential cover or two; Springsteen sometimes led vocals on versions of "My Generation" by the Who and "Mystic Eyes" by Them.

(Left) The Café Wha? in Greenwich Village was one of the venues where a young Springsteen, in the Castiles, learned his stage chops.

performing on *The Ed Sullivan Show*. Springsteen said of "The King" to his biographer Peter Ames Carlin, "He was actually the forerunner for a new kind of man. Everyone changed their ideas about *everything* after that. About race, about sex, about gender descriptions, what you could look like, what you could wear. It was outrageous. It's a fantastic thing to be." Springsteen just *had* to get a guitar the next day. Though he knew he looked different—i.e., *better*—with the acoustic guitar his mom had rented strapped around his young frame, his fingers were too small to negotiate its neck.

A few years later, the Beatles managed to do what Elvis couldn't; when Springsteen fell in love with them as a fourteen-year-old, he was a few years older, possessed a bit more maturity and patience, and, most importantly, had wider hands. The acoustic guitar he bought with money he made painting a relative's house was complemented by a tuition songbook.

The Kent electric guitar his mother bought him during Christmas of 1964 cost the then-considerable sum of $60 (about $600 today; she took out a loan). Perhaps it was partly determination not to waste precious family resources that led Springsteen to become a model guitar student (albeit self-taught), diligently practicing despite his father frequently shouting his objections.

Springsteen enrolled in community college but was clearly destined for a musical career. His first band was the Castiles, a local crew he joined at the age of fifteen. They were succeeded as berths by Earth, Steel Mill (née Child), Bruce Springsteen & the Friendly Enemies, the Sundance Band, Dr. Zoom & the Sonic Boom, Bruce Springsteen & the Hot Mammas, and the Bruce Springsteen Band. Initially limited to the role of guitarist, he quickly climbed to the position of songwriter, frontman, and eventually linchpin. It was his charisma and compositions that were the reason why Steel Mill could pull in audiences of up to four thousand without the benefit of a recording contract. It was possibly inevitable that he became torn between pursuing the band option and a singer-songwriter-style career, to which purpose he began dabbling in solo performances.

Not that he was ever doing anything in those days other than scratching a living. Although he often subsisted on pitiful income levels, it was never so pitiful that he ever needed to work a day job. The latter was crucially important to a man whose father had been enveloped by a dead-end job-related aura of unfulfillment and humiliation.

Nevertheless, a status beyond that subsistence level proved elusive, even though by the end of 1972 he had his best backing band yet in the shape of the six-man ensemble that

MIKE APPEL

Mike Appel was the dominant—or simply maybe loudest—part of the Appel-Cretecos axis. He had made a living since the late 1950s as a musician, songwriter, and producer. One might conclude that the low recognition of almost everyone for and with whom Appel had thus far worked (the Humbugs, the Camelots, Michael St. Shaw, Tex and the Chex, the Balloon Farm, Sir Lord Baltimore) marked him as a nonentity. His one notable success was significant, however: in the early 1970s he successfully placed five songs with the Partridge Family at a time when that imaginary TV pop group, who released very much nonimaginary hit records, were phenomenally successful. The Appel/Cretecos/Wes Farrell–written "Doesn't Somebody Want to Be Wanted" was a Cash Box #1.

The match hardly seemed ideal. Springsteen was perennially good-natured and modest while Appel was abrasive and self-aggrandizing. Columbia Records' John Hammond once commented, "Appel is as offensive as any man I've ever met." Yet the combination of a man too nice to push himself to the top and a manager too nasty to take no for an answer reaped dividends. "But he's utterly selfless in his devotion to Bruce," Hammond also noted.

Appel would be Springsteen's producer and manager for three albums before a bitter falling out and a lawsuit ended their professional relationship. After that, he plodded along in the same journeyman fashion that characterized his pre-Springsteen career. He had, however, done everything that a manager could conceivably be asked to do for his charge: discovered him, mentored him, and delivered him to the brink of superstardom.

Before he adopted Springsteen as a client, Mike Appel had achieved little as musician, producer, or songwriter. The one shining exception was his success in placing compositions with the Partridge Family. "Doesn't Somebody Want to Be Wanted" was a chart-topper.

Springsteen's first two albums had *something*, but it wasn't quite clear what. They enjoyed only modest success.

would eventually be named the E Street Band. The group—some members of which he had worked with before—played the type of synthesis of R&B, soul, and folk purveyed by Van Morrison. Things changed dramatically in 1971, though, when Springsteen came to the attention of Mike Appel and Jim Cretecos, contract songwriters who recently had moved into production and management.

Appel and Cretecos weren't overly impressed by Springsteen's audition but saw enough potential in him to suggest he get in touch again when he had more to show them. Whenhe spent a short holiday in California—where his parents and youngest sister had relocatedwhen he was entering his twenties—Springsteen's writing came on in such leaps and bounds that in February 1972 Appel and Cretecos decided to sign him to their newly formed Laurel Canyon production company.

By some combination of genius and chutzpah, by May 2 the hardly well-known, hardly mega-successful Appel had secured Springsteen an audition with the legendary John Hammond of Columbia Records. Springsteen was stunned. He recently had been reading Anthony Scaduto's *Bob Dylan*, the first proper biography of rock's greatest poet, in which Hammond played a key part.

JOHN HAMMOND

John Hammond was an artists and repertoire (A&R) man and producer at Columbia/CBS Records for, off and on, five decades. Like all A&R men, he had his share of failures and wrong hunches over the years, but few talent scouts could boast the glittering litany of discoveries he made across the course of his career.

Born in 1910, Hammond came from a privileged background—he was related to the Vanderbilt family, something that didn't stop him becoming a prominent civil rights activist. He was a musician himself but ventured professionally into journalism and deejaying before settling into his behind-the-scenes music industry role. Without John Hammond, the world may never have heard of not just Bruce Springsteen but also Count Basie, Bob Dylan, Aretha Franklin, Billie Holliday, Stevie Ray Vaughan, and many more titanic talents whom he championed when they were in the foothills of their careers.

His life was provided a perfect capstone in 1986 when he was inducted into the Rock and Roll Hall of Fame just one year before his death.

Several years before they met, Springsteen drew comparisons to Bob Dylan—another John Hammond discovery.

John Hammond was an A&R man and producer for Columbia/CBS Records and a legend in the music business. He helped discover many greats (including Springsteen) and in 1986 was deservedly inducted into the Rock and Roll Hall of Fame.

(Left) Springsteen emotes in a November 1974 performance at the Trenton War Memorial. *Born to Run* was just around the corner.

(Below) Springsteen enjoyed an early reputation as an electric live performer—although you wouldn't necessarily know it from this poster.

Hammond enjoyed the handful of songs Springsteen sang to him in his office. Once he'd seen him at an open-mic live performance and then secured the okay of company president Clive Davis, Springsteen duly became a Columbia recording artist. The rest is history? Hardly. In 1973, Springsteen released two albums, both produced by Appel and Cretecos. However, the albums did little more than make it clear that while Springsteen had *something*, he unfortunately didn't yet quite know what to do with it.

Springsteen has always been a dichotomy: insisting on being a solo artist but always desiring the company of a permanent backing band. His most famous one was named after a street in Belmar, New Jersey, where the mother of the E Street Band's keyboardist David Sancious lived.

For any other new recording artist, this wouldn't matter quite so much; it's understood after all that there's a learning curve and evolutionary process in the music biz like everywhere else. Unfortunately, when promoting Springsteen's debut album, *Greetings from Asbury Park, N.J.*, Columbia went big on the impression of a Bob Dylan resemblance and association created by Springsteen's poetic lyrics and the Hammond connection. At this stage, finding the "New Dylan" was considered in some quarters a crucial imperative simply because Dylan had vacated his throne and was currently in the middle of what would turn out to be a self-imposed three-year exile from meaningful recording, him simultaneously renouncing his de facto status as leader of the world's counterculture. Comparing someone just finding his feet as a songwriter and recording artist to a living legend with a vast back catalog of classic and revolutionary songs was a surefire way to create disappointment in anyone who bought Springsteen's likeable but unremarkable entrée.

Despite lackluster sales and reviews of *Greetings from Asbury Park, N.J.* and *The Wild, the Innocent and the E Street Shuffle*, Springsteen kept his spirits up and his faith in his own abilities alive.

It was also guaranteed to incur resentment in critics and DJs. Reviews of the LP ranged from lukewarm to hostile, and it initially sold a pitiful twenty-five thousand copies. The follow-up *The Wild, the Innocent and the E Street Shuffle* was received slightly more warmly and shifted slightly more units, but not enough to make the label's accountants perceive Springsteen as an asset.

GREETINGS FROM ASBURY PARK, N.J. (JANUARY 1973)

The overarching feel of Bruce Springsteen's debut is uncertain. The songs have consistently clever and interesting (if rambling) lyrics but often to no purpose. With few exceptions he's making no sociological or even personal statement but just annotating the passing parade. The songs on *Greetings from Asbury Park, N.J.* also show his tendency to unnecessary mythologize and stylize: He comes across as trading in gritty realism, but his characters have names like Wild Billy or G-Man instead of, well, Bruce or Steve. Meanwhile, the instrumentation is competent, sometimes slick, but too often a featureless clatter.

Song-wise, *Greetings* ranges from plodding ("Lost in the Flood") to likably breezy ("Does This Bus Stop at 82nd Street?") to something on the brink of greatness. In the latter category are the risqué, funkily anthemic "Blinded by the Light" and the sultry teen drama "Spirit in the Night." The true highlight is the lovely, spirited "Growin' Up," a song that examines adolescence with unusual vulnerability and self-critical modesty.

By late 1972, Springsteen was beginning to find his musical comrades in arms. From left are drummer Vini Lopez, organist Danny Federici, Springsteen, bassist Garry Tallent, and sax-wailing performance linchpin (and good friend) Clarence Clemons. Though this was not yet the definitive lineup of the E Street Band, Springsteen was set on the journey that would make him a peerless live act and international superstar.

Yet despite the underwhelming reception to that opening brace of albums, Springsteen and the E Street Band also were able to engender outsize goodwill because anyone who saw them in concert simply fell in love with them. They were building a reputation as one of the best stage acts in the United States courtesy of Springsteen's natural warmth and childlike enthusiasm, his self-deprecating and evocative autobiographical song preambles, and the mighty sonic wallop packed by the band named after the New Jersey road where the mother of keyboardist David Sancious lived. In fact, the power of Springsteen's live performances left observers bewildered as to why the same fun and fury wasn't found on his records; Charles Shaar Murray of Britain's *New Musical Express* opined, "It ain't possible to see his show and walk out quite the same. I mean, the cat is *good* . . ." but condemned Springsteen's releases as "dumb and irrelevant." Those in the know ached for Springsteen to capture on tape the transcendent qualities they'd borne witness to in the flesh. It was a trick contemporaneous band the Faces—superb live, mediocre in the studio—would never consistently manage. In 1974, it seemed that Springsteen was destined for the same fate.

In Asbury Park, Springsteen began to make a name for himself at venues like the Stone Pony.

THE WILD, THE INNOCENT AND THE E STREET SHUFFLE (NOVEMBER 1973)

Springsteen's second album was much more of an ensemble effort than his debut. Many long-term Springsteen fans consider it the LP most representative of any of his live acts, but this particular live act was a fleeting phenomenon. At this point, the E Street Band was not the ensemble of tight structures and high impact the world came to know and love but instead a group specializing in elasticity and improvisation.

The long and loose music on *The Wild, the Innocent and the E Street Shuffle* is accompanied by lyrics that show Springsteen developing his romanticized *West Side Story* version of street life. The three epics on side two of the album's original vinyl configuration verge on creating a new musical style, an amalgam of classical, rock, and jazz. Whether this concoction is any good is a different matter.

For instance, the ten-minute "New York City Serenade" is undeniably pretty and sometimes achieves a dreamlike ambience, but for all its tilts at profundity and musical elegance, it is ultimately inconsequential, a victim once again of the perennial fault of Springsteen's first two albums: lyrics with an unresolved air. His style is simply to jot down notes and make observations that never reach any meaningful conclusions.

A couple of songs hint at something more. "4th of July, Asbury Park (Sandy)" would be as lovely as its lilting guitars and sing-along melody seek to make it were it not so overlong. The plaintive and horny—and again lengthy—"Rosalita (Come Out Tonight)" has a rhythmic power and charm but again never quite crosses the bridge lying between ambition and achievement.

Springsteen strums a chord on his trusty Fender Telecaster while opening for Stevie Wonder at Kutztown State College on March 29, 1973.

Springsteen was a talented if unfocused songwriter early in his career. The street tableaux on his first two albums were vivid yet at the same time inconsequential, and they frustrated those critics who adored his live performances.

CITY
WARRIORS

2

MAKE OR BREAK: THE SESSIONS

Despite his robust club touring schedule and positive reviews of live performances, Columbia almost cut its losses with Bruce Springsteen before *Born to Run*. It was unclear that Springsteen and the E Street Band—in whatever form it took, like here with (from left) Peter Knobler, Greg Mitchell, Bruce Springsteen, and David Sancious—would ever be anything more than local sensations.

In an alternate universe, Bruce Springsteen's recording career sputtered to a permanent halt after eighteen months, with Columbia cutting its losses after his opening brace of low-selling albums, Springsteen left forever after telling anyone who cared to listen that he was once hailed as the New Dylan and that the underwhelming nature of the records he was briefly allowed to make were unrepresentative of his talents.

The reason for that possible outcome was that in the spring of 1974 his record company declined to fund a third album. Scraping a living with live appearances, he was at a loss as to where he could go next. That Springsteen was eventually able to snatch victory from the jaws of looming defeat and potential lifelong underachievement is due to dumb luck, deliberate calculation, and his own profound talent.

DAVID SANCIOUS

David Sancious was the only member of the E Street Band to actually live on the street that gave that ensemble its name. Born in 1953, Sancious became interested in music at age six when his family moved from Belmar to Asbury Park and found that the previous owners of their new house had left behind an unexpected bonus: an upright piano. In truth, he also enjoyed a bit of a head start: His mother was a proficient classical pianist.

In mid-1974, a Columbia Records A&R man told him he was impressed by a demo tape he'd made a couple of years earlier and wanted to sign him to a deal. Sancious had to seize the opportunity even though, "I knew for sure that Bruce was going to be huge." The latter impression was not exactly undermined by "Born to Run," the one track on the third album on which he did feature. His band, Tone, only released two albums, but it's doubtful Sancious has regretted leaving the E Streeters: If he hadn't, it's likely he would never have played keys for luminaries such as Jon Anderson, Jeff Beck, Jack Bruce, Eric Clapton, Peter Gabriel, and Sting. In 2019 he worked with Springsteen again, appearing on the album *Western Stars*.

David Sancious is a talented musician with many clients, performances, and tours to his name. This photo is from the Jack Bruce & Friends tour in 1980. Like Lopez, Sancious was also inducted into the Rock and Roll Hall of Fame in 2014 for his contributions to the E Street Band.

While recording *Born to Run*, Springsteen was obliged to continue playing gigs to keep body and soul together. Those people laying down their five-dollar admittance fee were helping to fund his breakthrough and, for many, masterpiece album.

Although his career had been only inching along, Springsteen was increasingly a perfectionist. This applied not merely to his songs but also to his band. Drummer Vini Lopez earned the nickname "Mad Dog" for a reason—his fiery temperament finally proved too much even for someone whom Max Weinberg, another Springsteen drummer, has described as the most patient man he has ever met. Before Weinberg secured the E Street Band drumming gig, there was a brief interregnum in which Ernest "Boom" Carter (a buddy of David Sancious) fulfilled the role from February 1974 after an audition at the home of bassist Garry Tallent's parents during a period in which the E Streeters constituted a remarkably multiethnic ensemble of three whites and three Blacks.

Meanwhile, the luck part of that turnaround triumvirate came in April when, talking to a reporter with the Brown University newspaper, Springsteen sounded off about Columbia's attitude toward him in the wake of the departure of their previous president Clive Davis. (He could have also mentioned that another reason for his recent feeling of friendlessness at the label was that John Hammond was gone as well.) "Now I'm a pain in the ass to them is all and, you know, they want to make somebody else famous," he lamented. Although the perennially good-natured Springsteen couldn't bring himself to bad-mouth Davis's successor Irwin Segelstein in print, someone who felt that criticism of him was implicit in his comments was Segelstein's son, who it so happened was both a Brown student and a Springsteen fan, and—according to Appel—rang his dad to remonstrate with him about his treatment of his hero. Thus alerted to Springsteen's public utterances of private disgruntlement, Segelstein arranged a meeting with Springsteen, Appel, and Appel's lawyer at which it was agreed that recording finances would be forthcoming for Springsteen to record again but there would be no more public bellyaching.

This *Rolling Stone* ad provided a glimpse for those who hadn't seen Landau's *Real Paper* rave, one of the most famous reviews of all time. "Springsteen does it all," Landau exclaimed. "There is no one I would rather watch on a stage today."

ROLLING STONE, JULY 18, 1974 3

"I SAW ROCK AND ROLL FUTURE AND ITS NAME IS BRUCE SPRINGSTEEN."

—Jon Landau

"...Tonight there is someone I can write of the way I used to write, without reservations of any kind. Last Thursday, at the Harvard Square Theatre, I saw my rock'n'roll past flash before my eyes. I saw something else: I saw rock and roll future and its name is Bruce Springsteen. And on a night when I needed to feel young, he made me feel like I was hearing music for the very first time.

"When his two-hour set ended I could only think, can anyone really be this good, can anyone say this much to me, can rock'n'roll still speak with this kind of power and glory? And then I felt the sores on my thighs where I had been pounding my hands in time for the entire concert and knew that the answer was yes.

"Springsteen does it all. He is a rock'n'roll punk, a Latin street poet, a ballet dancer, an actor, a joker, bar band leader, hot rhythm guitar player, extraordinary singer, and a truly great rock'n'roll composer. He leads a band like he has been doing it forever. I racked my brains but simply can't think of a white artist who does so many things so superbly. There is no one I would rather watch on a stage today.

"Bruce Springsteen is a wonder to look at. Skinny, dressed like a reject from Sha Na Na, he parades in front of his all-star rhythm band like a cross between Chuck Berry, early Bob Dylan, and Marlon Brando. Every gesture, every syllable adds something to his ultimate goal—to liberate our spirit while he liberates his by baring his soul through his music. Many try, few succeed, none more than he today.

"It's five o'clock now—I write columns like this as fast as I can for fear I'll chicken out —and I'm listening to 'Kitty's Back.' I do feel old but the record and my memory of the concert has made me feel a little younger. I still feel the spirit and it still moves me.

"I bought a new home this week and upstairs in the bedroom is a sleeping beauty who understands only too well what I try to do with my records and typewriter. About rock'n'roll, The Lovin' Spoonful once sang, 'I'll tell you about the magic that will free your soul / But it's like trying to tell a stranger about rock'n'roll.' Last Thursday I remembered that the magic still exists and that as long as I write about rock, my mission is to tell a stranger about it— just as long as I remember that I'm the stranger I'm writing for."—***Jon Landau, The Real Paper, May 22, 1974.***

Bruce Springsteen's second album, "The Wild, the Innocent and the E Street Shuffle." On Columbia Records

BRUCE SPRINGSTEEN: THE WILD, THE INNOCENT & THE E STREET SHUFFLE
including:
Rosalita (Come Out Tonight)/Incident On 57th Street
Kitty's Back/Wild Billy's Circus Story
4th Of July, Asbury Park (Sandy)

Also available on tape

The calculation portion of Springsteen's rebirth was not actually scheming on his part but that of two well-placed fans, Dave Marsh and Jon Landau. They were music journalists at a point in pre-internet history when the power of print could make, break, or (in this case) revitalize an artist, even the lesser power of a counterculture weekly paper distributed in the Boston area. The very month after the Brown University newspaper feature, these two Springsteen fans and staffers of Boston's The Real Paper conspired to run a laudatory piece about Springsteen with the aim of alleviating Springsteen's troubles with his label. Landau's eulogizing of Springsteen in his "Loose Ends" column headlined "Growing Young with Rock and Roll" that appeared in the May 22, 1974, issue had the desired impact and more.

Before Max Weinberg cemented his role as the E Street Band's main drummer, it was Vini "Mad Dog" Lopez's gig. In between came Ernest "Boom" Carter, whose sole contribution to *Born to Run* was the title track.

Of the nearly two thousand words Landau wrote, almost two-thirds were spent detailing his history with music as consumer, failed musician, sometime record producer, and critic, and how that journey had seen him become increasingly disillusioned with rock. In his column, Landau summed his malcontent up in several ways: partly because of the different priorities and responsibilities that come with growing older; partly because of the detachment that goes with analyzing it for a living; and—implied more than said—partly because of an overall decline in the quality of music. Finally, he got to the artist whose concert at the Harvard Square Theatre in Cambridge, Massachusetts, on May 9 he had the pleasure to witness: "But tonight there is someone I can write of the way I used to write, without reservations of any kind. Last Thursday . . . I saw my rock'n'roll past flash before my eyes. And I saw something else: I saw rock and roll future and its name is Bruce Springsteen. And on a night when I needed to feel young, he made me feel like I was hearing music for the very first time. . . . I could only think, can anyone really be this good; can anyone say this much to me, can rock'n'roll still speak with this kind of power and glory? . . . Springsteen does it all. He is a rock'n'roll punk, a Latin street poet, a ballet dancer, an actor, a joker, bar band leader, hot-shit rhythm guitar player, extraordinary singer, and a truly great rock'n'roll composer. . . . There is no one I would rather watch on a stage today."

ERNEST "BOOM" CARTER

An Asbury Park native and multi-instrumentalist born in 1952, Ernest "Boom" Carter acquired his nickname as a teenager when police arrived at his house after reports of shots fired and found it was actually him whacking his drum kit. Post-Springsteen, he went on to play with the likes of Southside Johnny and the Asbury Jukes, Lance Larson, Billy Hector, Billy Squier, and Steve Forbert. He also set up a music production company named Niblack Productions.

Carter's one and only contribution to the Springsteen canon is impressive: his propulsive sticks work on "Born to Run" (the track). His jazzy, syncopated fill in the instrumental section is one that even a master like Max Weinberg could never replicate.

He has no regrets about leaving the E Streeters. "It put me on the map, and I'm so proud to think about it," he told *Asbury Park Press* in 2014.

Some performers are just innately charismatic. Springsteen strikes a typically mesmerizing pose despite probably being oblivious of how dramatic the lights were making him look.

When he was "Growin' Up," no one—least of all Springsteen—could have predicted what the 1970s would hold for this New Jersey boy.

It's slightly disappointing that such stirring rhetoric is not what it seems—a spontaneous outpouring of epiphanic awe—but, rather, cold-blooded manipulation. Nonetheless, history will forever record the Machiavellian scheming behind the review—possibly the most famous in the history of music journalism—as the right thing to do. Right not just because of the justice of the two men's cause but because, more importantly, it worked. In July, the label that had cut in half the budget for Springsteen's second album from that for his debut was happy to launch a $50,000 publicity campaign (more than $300,000 in today's coinage) to trumpet the same album's merits, part of which was a full-page, page-three ad in *Rolling Stone* in which it reprinted a large chunk of Landau's *Real Paper* write-up, headlined with the quotation-marked words, "I saw rock and roll future and its name is Bruce Springsteen."

There may be cause to question Appel's assertion that the Segelstein intervention constituted some kind of corporate backing down: The sequence of events suggests that Columbia stuck to its insistence that allowing Springsteen to record a new album was contingent on providing a single first. Springsteen was at least on Columbia's radar again, however, and Appel's contention that it eventually led to a switch to a better studio seems plausible.

The single idea, though, had always been a bizarre one. It's true that Springsteen was a man weaned on singles, not just because he was a kid in the 1960s when 45 rpm was king, but also because there was no record player in his house until he was thirteen or fourteen and his only soundtrack was AM radio. From the get-go, however, Bruce Springsteen was clearly an albums artist. The 1970s was a point at which serious musicians began to view the hit parade as a side issue while the album was gaining preeminent status, not least because it was increasingly within the purchasing power of consumers. Springsteen's music and profile and the way Columbia had always marketed him chimed with this zeitgeist. It's possible that Columbia's stipulation was a hedge-betting exercise if not an outright ruse—if Springsteen failed to deliver a song for 45-rpm release that did not fulfill some criteria known only to the label, it could jettison him with minimum fuss. Judging by his public comments, Springsteen seemed to suspect this.

Acoustic 370

Back-to-back or side by side, Clemons and Springsteen were the fulcrum of a mighty collective stage experience. However, whether the acknowledged live prowess of the E Street Band could translate to a recording was something that needed to be determined by *Born to Run*.

This is where Springsteen's brilliance entered the equation. He went on something of a journey during the making of the "Born to Run" single. It started as a resented chore, yet he quickly came to a decision that, if he *was* going to be forced to record a single, he would make "the greatest rock record I'd ever heard." The unintended consequence of this was that it forced upward the quality level of the subsequent album. Even if one doesn't subscribe to the idea that with "Born to Run" he actually achieved his mission of creating the greatest rock single of all time, few will dispute that the recording is remarkable in its aspiration, production, skill, and power. It would have been immediately obvious to Springsteen that he could hardly stick a track of such grandeur on an album with songs that were "merely" of his previous standard. An additional issue was that said album had to facilitate his commercial breakthrough. From that song's inception, the *Born to Run* album was forged in scope and ambition; however bizarre the single diktat, it could be argued that it was the best thing to ever happen to Springsteen.

The location where Springsteen set about trying to achieve his bold ambition was somewhat incongruous; 914 Sound Studios in New York is not exactly up there with Abbey Road, Gold Star, or Mussel Shoals as a recording venue where magic has been made. Then again, it was designed to be cheap. Founded in 1970 by Arthur Brodsky, Phil Ramone, Art Ward, and Don Frey, its location in Blauvelt, 20 miles (32 km) outside of New York City, meant that while it wasn't as handy as NYC studios, its prices were commensurately lower. Its clientele was never meant to be top-tier artists: Janis Ian and Dusty Springfield had recorded there, but that was pretty much the beginning and end of its list of illustrious clients. Its out-of-the-way location was not the only reason for this, but also its dull acoustics and outdated equipment (a resident piano with a squeaky pedal was a particular bone of contention with artists). Springsteen had managed to get reasonable results when recording his first two albums there, however, and the financial circumstances

The innocuous cum shabby 914 Sound Studios was located 20 miles (32 km) outside of New York City. Dusty Springfield and Janis Ian had recorded there, and Springsteen had carved the guts of "Born to Run" within its modest environs, but a better venue was necessary for Springsteen's increasingly grandiose visions.

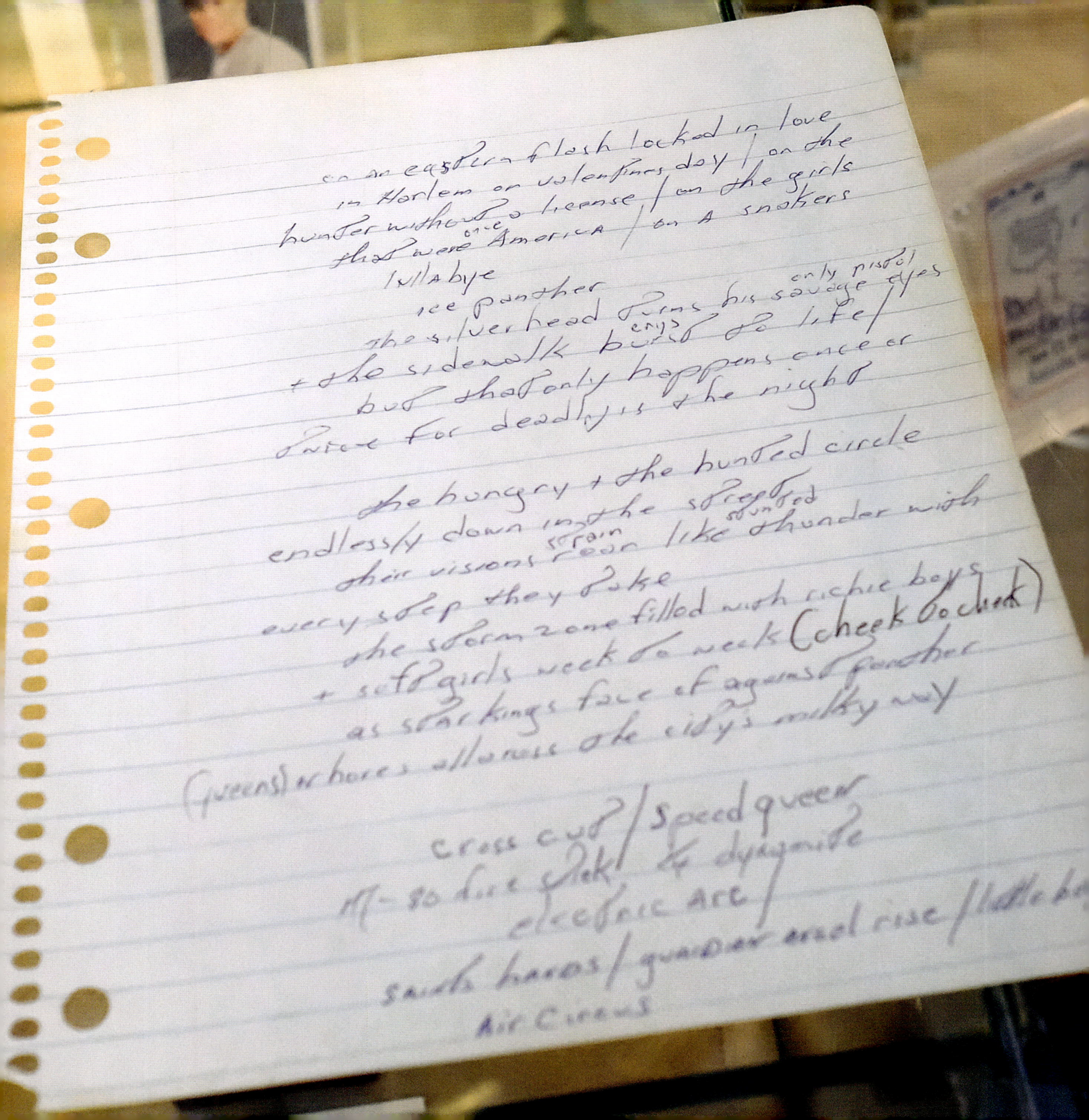
on an eastern flash locked in love
in Harlem on valentines day / on the
hunter without a license / on the girls
that were once America / on A smokers
lullabye
ice panther
only pistol
the silverhead turns his savage eyes
crys
+ the sidewalk burst to life /
but that only happens once or
twice for deadly is the night
the hungry + the hunted circle
endlessly down in the streets
sounded
strain
their visions roar like thunder with
every step they take
the storm zone filled with richie boys
+ soft girls week to week (cheek to cheek)
as starkings face of against panther
(queens) whores allowance the city's milky way
cross cut / speed queen
M-80 fire stick / & dynamite
electric arc /
saints hands / guardian angel rise / little b
Air Circus

"Born to Run" will always be the album's most famous track, but closer "Jungleland" arguably tops it. Here are some of its handwritten lyrics in an early stage of the song; "the hungry and the hunted" is a familiar component, but other lines didn't make it to the final studio version.

(Right) This 1974 poster might boast that Springsteen was a Columbia recording artist, but by this point the label was beginning to wish he wasn't. The preamble to *Born to Run* marked a period during which Springsteen was fighting to maintain credibility with Columbia.

that had dictated the choice of 914 in the first place were still operative.

"Born to Run" was a grand statement both words- and music-wise. Its lyric is the assertion of a low-born man that moving away as fast as physically possible from his insalubrious environs is the only possible salvation open to him. The high drama of its melody and instrumentation is bolstered by its towering production. For all the 914 studio's faults, it rose to the objectives and challenges Springsteen, Appel, and recording engineer Louis Lahav posed it from May 21, 1974, over an approximate three months, even if the track wasn't finalized there.

It also must be said that when Columbia was presented with a rough mix of the song in August, it was not as impressed by the results as Springsteen and Appel intended. In a memo to his client, Appel lamented that the label had taken "lightly" the recording they had slaved over. Nonetheless, Springsteen had delivered a single as stipulated, and it furthermore was that farthest thing imaginable from a phoned-in pop song; the combination of that and Springsteen's friends in the press—and quite possibly the nagging of Irwin Segelstein's son—seems to have combined to ensure that Columbia now felt obliged to allow Springsteen and company to enter a recording studio once more with the specific purpose of creating a long player. Nonetheless, a sword of Damocles continued to hang over Springsteen: The results of these sessions absolutely could not be another flop album.

August 1, 1974, is the momentous date when the *Born to Run* album sessions properly got underway. The single was still not quite finished, nor was "So Young and in Love," the song that was, in the sense that they had started recording life together, its mate. Those would be subject to further work that day along with another song—"Jungleland"—of which there were a couple of stabs, one of which resulted in a complete take.

It had been obvious that "Jungleland" was something special from its onstage debut in July 1974, although the song's evolution took it down a few wrong turns—including the dubious early title "Calvin (Little Jesus) Jones and the 13th Apostle"—and a stage where it was more akin to jazz-rock or even prog rock before ending up in the form it did.

STUDER
MULTICHANNEL TAPE RECORDER A800
PLAY
STOP
REC
EDIT

(Left) Music production technology was making leaps and bounds in the 1970s. Nonetheless, Springsteen's perfectionism meant that *Born to Run* was a far from easy album to make.

(Below) In the 1970s, albums such as *Tommy*, *Quadrophenia*, and *The Wall* offered listeners not just songs but extended narratives. Clemons suspected Springsteen's "Magic Rat" character may have sprung from similar "rock opera" ambitions.

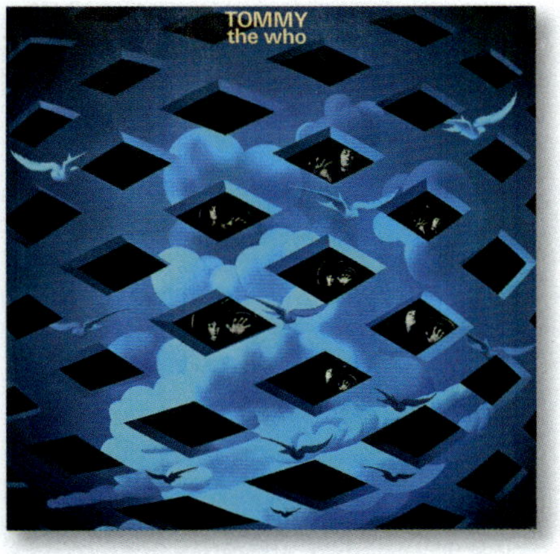

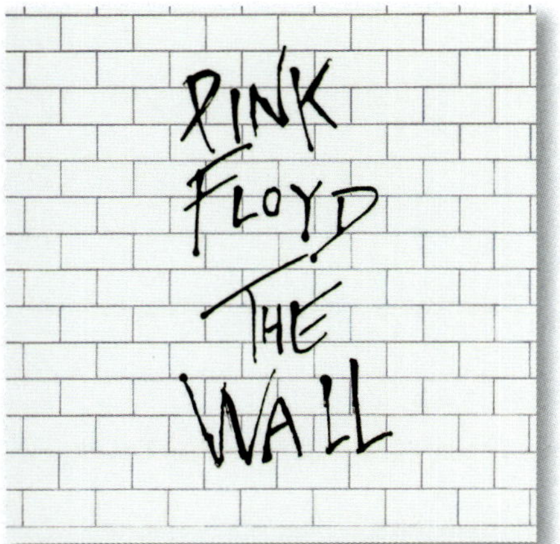

Suggestions that *Born to Run* was at one point intended to be a concept album seem to revolve around this song. Clemons wrote in his 2009 autobiography *Big Man*, "In the beginning, I think Bruce was going for a rock opera kind of thing about this character called Magic Rat. He had lots of songs and themes that were built around the narrative he had in his head. Eventually, he let that go." Some credence is given to Clemons's interpretation by a spring 1974 rough track listing that indicated at least one vinyl side of the proposed third album would be dedicated to a "Jungleland" suite consisting of "From the Churches to the Jails," "The Hungry & the Hunted," "Between Flesh & Fantasy," and "Jungleland," albeit with the older song "Zero and Blind Terry" thrown in too. Eventually, "Jungleland" became just one (admittedly long) song in which Magic Rat was central.

Nonetheless, Springsteen indeed formulated a concept for the album. It was the type of concept that has informed almost all his albums since and is frankly not fully comprehensible to anyone who's not Bruce Springsteen, but roughly speaking it amounts to a depiction of a group of characters going through a broadly similar life experience in a narrow geographical location and time frame. Whatever the extent or coherency of that album concept, the overall title for it changed repeatedly. Its several identities included *War and Roses*, *The Hungry and the Hunted*, *American Summer*, and *Sometimes at Night* before finally becoming *Born to Run*.

August 3 saw no recording work because the band was booked to play Central Park as support to Anne Murray. They went down a storm—better apparently than the headliner—but neither that nor the fact that they had been heavily reliant on gig money in recent times prevented them then canceling all gigs over the coming ten days to concentrate on recording. A difficulty had arisen with the announcement that Sancious and—no sooner than he had joined—Carter were leaving the E Street Band to launch their own recording careers. Springsteen now had to rebuild the group just when he was trying to salvage his career with a make-or-break LP. He sought to make the most of their notice period and knuckled down to completing what he had in the can.

A usable basic track of "Born to Run" had existed since May, and it had been garnished with a vocal in late June. In keeping with his belated ambition to make it an all-time classic to end all-time classics, Springsteen wanted to build on what he had, and build high. The grandiosity he desired preceded—even precipitated—the song itself. Mike Appel told Clinton Heylin circa 2012, "Bruce says, 'I want my records to sound like Phil Spector.'" Appel advised Springsteen that, if that was his wish, his songs needed to be very different from his usual fare. As Appel noted to David Horovitz of the *Times of Israel* in 2016,

PHIL SPECTOR

"Little symphonies for the kids." The famous descriptive quote from Phil Spector perfectly summarized the "Wall of Sound" pop production style he pioneered.

Born in 1939, Spector became a hitmaker when still a teenager when he wrote the Teddy Bears' US #1, "To Know Him Is to Love Him." He quickly added to his bow the strings of producer and label owner. Alighting on the technique of generating power by having multiple sets of instruments playing at once and frequently adding classical string and woodwind overdubs as well as oodles of reverb, he employed it on a line of transatlantic hits, many of which instantly became iconic, including "Da Doo Ron Ron" by the Crystals, "Be My Baby" by the Ronettes, and "You've Lost That Lovin' Feelin'" by the Righteous Brothers.

Spector never really recovered from an ill-considered abortive retirement prompted by his fury that "River Deep, Mountain High"—a soaring 1966 Ike and Tina Turner single that he was convinced was his masterpiece—was not the hit he thought it should have been.

His genius always coexisted with disturbing personality traits that included obsessions with control and guns. His life reached the denouement that in hindsight always seemed inevitable when in 2009 he was convicted of the 2003 murder of actress Lana Clarkson. He died in prison in 2021.

Spector was responsible for many iconic, larger-than-life hits, including "Da Doo Ron Ron" by the Crystals and "You've Lost That Lovin' Feelin'" by the Righteous Brothers. Springsteen wanted that sort of towering ambience for *Born to Run*.

Phil Spector was a legendary producer for decades. He created the "Wall of Sound" production style that influenced many musicians, both successful ones and wannabes like the young Bruce Springsteen.

"I said, . . . 'On a Phil Spector recording, there's maybe 30 words in the whole song. You have 130 on every song. So, for you to pare down your lyrics to the point where you can actually be doing musical production values, something's gotta give here.'" Appel was highly skeptical that Springsteen could manage this feat, but when Springsteen turned in "Born to Run," he found that it was spare like nothing he'd ever heard from him. This may be the most remarkable fact about the *Born to Run* album, for it means that Springsteen had the discipline and craft to change his writing style virtually overnight. The verbose wordplay found on his first two albums—and which secured him a recording deal in the first place—was something to which he would never return.

Springsteen told *Melody Maker*'s Michael Watts shortly after the song's completion, "We approached the record the way that some of the early sixties producers like Phil Spector or Brian Wilson would approach their records, which is to create this *sound*. It's sort of an extreme record. . . . I wanted to make a *big* record. . . . No holds barred!"

Well, up to a point. Remarkably, the finished "Born to Run" was actually *smaller* than it had been at one point—synthesizers, classical strings, and horn charts at various junctures inhabited its topography. By the mid-1970s, technology had advanced as far as sixteen-track recording, but a many-layered production like this one still necessitated "bouncedowns," with resultant sound degradation. On an aesthetic level, Springsteen was overloading the sonic soundscape, oppressing the listener's ears. Eventually, much of the overlay was simply wiped away like so much windshield gunk.

(Left) When he lost two band members, there was no question of Springsteen replacing them with sessioners to complete Born to Run. Instead, he held several dozen tryouts before recruiting permanent replacements Max Weinberg on drums and Roy Bittan on piano.

(Right) Before his tragically early death in 2008, Danny Federici went back further with Springsteen as a bandmate than any other colleague. However, he is only found on *Born to Run*'s eponymous track. Federici began playing accordion at age seven after seeing it on *The Lawrence Welk Show*. His switch to the instrument on which he would find fame, organ, occurred when he realized that the Cordovox accordion could be turned on its side and played as a keyboard.

There was no question of drafting in sessioners in Carter's and Sancious's stead. As Springsteen told Jerry Gilbert of *Zigzag* in August 1974, "I don't like too many outside people involved. It just gets too impersonal." Instead, a classified was placed in *The Village Voice* to recruit replacements. The advertisement read, "Drummer (no jr. Ginger Bakers, must encompass R&B and jazz), pianist (classical to Jerry Lee Lewis), trumpet (must play r&b, Latin & jazz), violinist. All must sing. Male or female." As well as dubious grammar, the ad was replete with irony. The Latin and jazz capacities on which it insisted might have been strains in the E Street Band's sound before but in fact would pretty much disappear from this point forward as Springsteen became a far more orthodox rock artist. No trumpeter was subsequently recruited, and although Louis Lahav's wife Suki successfully auditioned for the violinist role, said instrument would not make the graduation from feature of the stage act to element of recordings.

When it comes to the drummer and pianist roles, Springsteen held sixty auditions, thirty for each vacancy. When at the end of them Max Weinberg became the E Street Band's drummer and Roy Bittan its pianist, the ensemble had profoundly changed—David Sancious and Clarence Carter were capable musicians, but the duo who replaced them were remarkably talented and polished. The old E Streeters were a bit funky and a bit unfocused, at least on disc. This tweaked aggregation was brawny and propulsive but also elegant.

JON LANDAU

Springsteen's wish for Jon Landau to act as coproducer was, for some, bizarre: Landau was a journalist. Though he had some experience as a music producer, that experience was limited, and it included *Back in the USA* (1970), the second album by leftist hard-rock act the MC5. While some people revere that work as an incendiary piece of proto-punk, others despise it as an antiseptic betrayal of the MC5's fearsome power.

Born in New York in 1947, Landau moved to Boston at age twelve. He busted into the birth of serious rock criticism, writing for *Crawdaddy* and then *Rolling Stone* from its very first issue.

Landau and Springsteen have been joined at the hip since the mid-1970s. Like Appel before him, he became Springsteen's producer happily but his manager reluctantly. Though he stepped back from producing his client in 1992, his stewardship of Springsteen business affairs continues to this day. Nor is he a one-hit management wonder: Other careers he has steered include that of Shania Twain.

Jon Landau wasn't a producer, musician, or manager by trade—he was a writer, one who appeared in the first issue of *Rolling Stone.* Landau continues to manage Springsteen today.

It was also—initially—minus Danny Federici. The long-serving E Street organist is found on *Born to Run* only on the title track. Bittan's penchant for tight structure initially unnerved and dismayed the extemporization-inclined Federici, and in his absence from the studio Bittan was left to overdub the organ parts. Federici returned to the fold for the tour to promote the album. Even without Federici's input, it was clear that the recalibrated E Street Band was something special, though that didn't automatically translate to spectacular progress in the studio. Only halting forward momentum was made when sessions commenced with the newbies in October. This may have been partly due to the fact that some of the material on which they were working was slight: Unlike all subsequent Springsteen albums, *Born to Run* did not produce high-quality outtakes.

Even though the core of the material was undeniably strong, the sessions were bitty and aimless and did not bode well for an album that had to convince Columbia that Springsteen was a fixture of its roster with a rosy future and persuade the wider world that this was a truly substantial artist. True, the crew had a truly great completed song in the can—and copies of "Born to Run" sneaked by Appel to sympathetic radio stations had apprised the public of its existence and Springsteen continuing viability—but the record company had now decided it didn't want to release a single yet, whether it was because they were waiting for the full album, because they were irritated at Appel for undermining them by playing to the gallery by leaking it, or because it had all been a Machiavellian ruse to ask him to record it in the first place. The group's focus also was broken to the extent that they had to end their gigging hiatus to pay their day-to-day bills. By August they had recorded only 20 nights out of a possible 123 across four months. "We're at the lowest we've ever been right now," Springsteen vouchsafed to *Zigzag*'s Gilbert. David Bowie was recording a couple of early Springsteen songs ("It's Hard to Be a Saint in the City" and "Growin' Up"), but the potential revenue from that was a distant possibility (and, as it turned out, Bowie wouldn't release them for a decade and a half). Jim Cretecos, for one, saw no future in all this and announced his shares in Springsteen Inc. were available to whoever wanted to buy them. The amount involved—$1,500—was small even in 1974, but Appel couldn't afford it, and one Jules Curz stepped in. Appel was only able to buy Curz's interest after six months or so.

With six months having passed with only scant progress, Springsteen concluded that the problem lay on the production side. This was not necessarily a slight on Appel—Springsteen was the LP's coproducer, and it naturally followed that if something was wrong, he was partly to blame. He concluded that a third man was needed on the production team, however, and that last part of the triumvirate was logically Jon Landau.

I DON'T
KNOW

Landau's tee may read "I don't know," but as far as Springsteen was concerned, he did: He credited his new producer with getting *Born to Run* out of the quagmire into which it had sunk.

Logical to him, anyway. Appel detested Landau's production work on the MC5's *Back in the USA* and—never backward in coming forward—told Landau so the first time they met. This may have been prompted by the fact that Landau had made disparaging comments in print about his coproduction of the first two Springsteen albums. Springsteen had taken note of those very same comments, however, and a month before Landau's rock'n'roll–future review, Springsteen had met the critic outside Charlie's Place in Boston, where the E Street Band were booked and where Landau's review of his second album had been placed in the window to attract punters. Spotting Springsteen reading it, Landau introduced himself and a relationship started. Springsteen sent him a cassette of the developing "Born to Run" track and eventually invited him in to watch an album session.

Landau visited 914 in February 1975. When Springsteen took him aside and asked him what he thought, Landau told him that in a particular segment of "Jungleland" the drummer and the bass player kept making the same mistake every time. This and various other Landau observations and suggestions confirmed Springsteen's belief that he could provide valuable input, and he asked Appel if he might come aboard. Appel reluctantly agreed, with part of his reluctance stemming from the fact that it would put he and Springsteen further into debt: Columbia would agree to pick up only 50 percent of Landau's producer fee. For his part, Landau had to quit his job at *Rolling Stone* to be able to devote the necessary time to his new role.

In April 1975, Landau effected one significant change—to relocate the sessions from 914 to the Record Plant, 321 West 44th Street, New York. Founded by Gary Kellgren and Chris Stone in 1968, the Record Plant was the foundation of what was now a country-wide chain, it having established California branches in 1969 (Los Angeles) and 1972 (Sausalito). The pair had sold the NYC branch to finance the California outlets, but the new owners had maintained the ethos that had gained it its prestigious reputation: an informal atmosphere appropriate to the libertarian ethos of rock music. Hand-in-hand with that approach was a genuine respect for popular music that meant that the studio was always happy to invest in the latest technological advances. Notable works already laid down, in whole or in part, at the Record Plant included the Jimi Hendrix Experience's *Electric Ladyland* (1968), John Lennon's *Imagine* (1971), Don McLean's *American Pie* (1971), Alice Cooper's *School's Out* (1972), and Aerosmith's *Get Your Wings* (1974).

The corollary of a studio at which the music aristocracy desired to record was, of course, top-tier pricing. Appel had negotiated from Columbia a budget increase of around $10,000 from the first two LPs' $40,000. Springsteen had recorded those albums quickly, though, and *Born to Run* marked the point at which Springsteen's

It is rumored that Suki Lahav moved to Israel with her husband to save her marriage after she and Springsteen became enamored with each other. Lahav contributed violin to "Jungleland" and decades later would tour with Springsteen.

Sessions for *Born to Run* relocated to New York's Record Plant. Legendary albums such as *Electric Ladyland*, *Imagine*, and *Get Your Wings* were recorded there in whole or in part.

"Build Your Own Future" reads some graffiti on the side of what used to be the legendary New York Record Plant studio. When the *Born to Run* sessions relocated there, Springsteen did just that.

perfectionism entered full swing. In subsequent years that would manifest itself in a protracted process of sifting. In this instance, the problem wasn't so much agonizing over which tracks to select but instead endless lyric rewriting, recording, and overdubbing, all overlaid with a purism about organicness. Bittan recalled to the *Austin Chronicle* in 2009, "Bruce didn't want to just splice the song together; we would perform it from beginning to end and try to get one great take—not easy to do. So there was a lot of rehearsal involved, a lot of construction." "We went over budget in about two seconds," Appel acidly wrote of the move to the Record Plant in his 1992 memoir *Down Thunder Road*.

Following a brief stop-off at Columbia Studios, New York, on March 17, when Appel, Springsteen, and Lahav had a go at remixing "Born to Run," sessions at the Record Plant began on April 18. That Lahav was unable to follow the project to the new studio was not because he was tied to 914, but because the previous month, he and his wife Suki had decamped to their native Israel. During Suki's short time with the E Street Band, she and Springsteen had—according to Appel—become smitten with each other and she had fled to save her marriage. Suki's violin can be heard on the released "Jungleland," a tiny, solitary piece of distaff influence on the recorded work of the pre–Patti Scialfa E Street Band.

It meant that the recalibrated production team of Appel/Landau/Springsteen was assisted by a new recording engineer. That Jimmy Iovine had not long ago finished working

Before adopting his now-iconic bandanas, Steven Van Zandt sported a more conservative and classic look. Here, he performs with Garry Tallent (left) and Roy Bittan (right) in 1975 at Alex Cooley's Electric Ballroom in Atlanta.

with John Lennon on his 1974 *Walls and Bridges* album might make it sound like he had a strong pedigree, but in fact Iovine was barely into his twenties and the half-dozen credits he had to his name were mostly as assistant engineer and mixing assistant. In other words, he was less practiced at production than the hardly veteran trio of Appel, Landau, and Springsteen. As Iovine noted in 1987 of the *Born to Run* sessions, "God, it was hard. . . . All of us were very young and inexperienced, so we had to go the long way to do anything."

There was arguably an uncredited fourth producer on *Born to Run*. Guitarist Steven Van Zandt was for Springsteen—his best pal since teendom—always a welcome presence in the studio. He was also the kind of character prepared to offer opinions and suggestions, wanted or not, outsider or no. Even Appel was happy with Van Zandt's role, and not necessarily because it was unpaid. "They needed direction and he gave it to them," he told Heylin. A case in point is "Tenth Avenue Freeze-Out," first attempted on May 5. Randy Brecker (trumpet, bugle), Michael Brecker (tenor saxophone), Dave Sanborn (baritone saxophone), and Wayne Andre (trombone) were audibly fine players, but at the time they were at a loss as to what to play on the song. With Appel making noises about postponing the session, Van Zandt intervened. Used to the dynamics of brass instruments through his work with Southside Johnny and the Asbury Jukes, he suggested that the musicians render lines that he proceeded to hum to them. The result was a quite glittering and enervating horn chart. For his part, Springsteen feels that the most important contribution Van Zandt made to the album—and indeed his entire career—was a suggestion he made to tweak his "Born to Run" guitar riff, thereby optimizing that famous vibrato-drenched Dick Dale–style motif.

(Rght) *Born to Run* engineer Jimmy Iovine (far right) had almost zero significant studio experience. Working for John Lennon as a low-level technician during the recording of *Walls and Bridges* was about the pinnacle of his achievements so far.

Many recording artists in the "progressive" 1970s lunged for the option of a wrenching guitar break. Springsteen preferred a haunting saxophone solo from Clarence Clemons for the musical interlude of "Jungleland."

Suggestions that the *Born to Run* album took anything up to twenty-one months to record are erroneous, brought about by what was then an inordinately long gap since the artist's previous album, the conflation of the off-and-on recording span with the actual time spent laying down parts, the participants' impressionistic memories of that frustratingly staccato recording process, and pained recollections of an ultra-finicky approach to perfecting tracks. The latter is demonstrated by a reminiscence from Springsteen that one evening Landau went missing from the studio after wordlessly walking out when yet again Springsteen couldn't make up his mind about a track's sonics. To make matters worse, it wasn't as if Landau or anyone else could reason with the artist. Springsteen might have been in the last-chance saloon, yet in spite of that fact (or perhaps because of it), he felt he had nothing to lose. As Iovine said to *Rolling Stone*'s David Fricke in 2012, "This guy was broke. You couldn't borrow him, rent him, get him to compromise. He didn't give a fuck who you were, what you were going to give him, it was him and that record."

Springsteen himself later sometimes gave the impression of believing the marathon-sessions myth. In a comment he made to his first biographer Dave Marsh in which he recalled living with his girlfriend in a Holiday Inn during the album's recording: "She says to me—she says it every night when I come home—'Is it finished?'" The reality is that while October 1974 through March 1975 was a time of little or no work on the record, studio logs indicate that by mid-April 1975 the sessions had finally eased out of that desultory stage lamented by Appel in his 103-lost-days memo and that steady work was achieved thereafter. Even then, the schedule was nothing like daily. Only July saw truly intensive work as Springsteen raced to complete the album before the start of the tour intended to promote it. At the end of the album, he was overdubbing a vocal to "She's the One" in one studio, mixing "Jungleland" in another, and rehearsing the band for their tour commencing July 20 in a third. Springsteen was remembering less emotively and more realistically than in the Marsh quote when he undramatically noted to DJ Dave Herman of the cumulative time expended, "It didn't take that long, actually. *Born to Run*, the album, was recorded in about four months."

By early July, Landau and Springsteen had become so tight and Springsteen's relationship with Appel so strained that the latter was effectively banned from the studio. In Appel's recollection, their arguments revolved around the album's final track listing, with him arguing vociferously—quite possibly, given his reputation, obnoxiously—against Springsteen's insistence on omitting "Meeting Across the River" and including the slight "Lonely Night in the Park" and "Linda Let Me Be the One." Appel claims his banishment

Springsteen had a vision for *Born to Run* from which he—with his career dependent on its success—would not deviate. In an interview in *Rolling Stone* in 2012, engineer Jimmy Iovine said, "This guy was broke. You couldn't borrow him, rent him, get him to compromise."

led to something of a crisis, however, and that Springsteen virtually begged him to come back. The main problem revolved around the fact that Springsteen had no confidence in the final track listing that had been decided on in Appel's absence. It's easy to understand why:

Side One

Thunder Road

Tenth Avenue Freeze-Out

Lonely Night in the Park

Jungleland

Night

Side Two

Linda Let Me Be the One

Meeting Across the River

She's the One

Backstreets

Yes, you read that right. "Born to Run" was not projected as part of the package. Springsteen clearly had lost sight of it after the million-and-one times he'd had to listen to it or component parts of it in his quest to perfect the track. If the upshot of Springsteen asking Appel to come back to the studio was the restoration of what would become the title track to his third album, his signature song, and a recording acclaimed across the world to this day, he owes his ex-manager a debt of gratitude that can never be repaid. Less important but also wise was the dropping of the unremarkable and unfocused "Lonely Night in the Park" and the slightly juvenile and repetitive "Linda Let Me Be the One." A more minor but still significant consequence of Appel being recalled was that the reconfigured contents enabled a symmetrical four tracks per side, thus giving each of them an equal footing and hence the patina of a statement. A rejigging that included placing "Jungleland" at the close of proceedings—surely its only logical place—was the final selection/sequencing masterstroke.

During the *Born to Run* tour, Springsteen and the E Street Band performed a five-night, ten-show residency at the Bottom Line in Greenwich Village that Columbia carefully packed with media people.

Other songs attempted at the *Born to Run* sessions seem to have never seriously been considered for inclusion, even if they sometimes appeared on the rough track listings Springsteen was in the habit of periodically drawing up. One is "So Young and in Love," a recording of course that dated as far back as "Born to Run." It's good fun but that itself would have made it a bit out of place on such a stern-browed work as *Born to Run*. "Janey Needs a Shooter" is a quite harrowing song that uses medical and violent metaphors to convey a narrator's desire to protect a woman. It dates from 1973 and was played at least once during the *Born to Run* sessions. Springsteen cowrote a different version of the song with Warren Zevon on Zevon's 1980 album *Bad Luck Streak in Dancing School*; Springsteen returned to "Janey Needs a Shooter" during sessions for *The River* but didn't release his own version of it until 2020 on *Letter to You*. Several other miscellaneous compositional fragments and rough song drafts recorded or considered during the *Born to Run* recording process were cannibalized by Springsteen for the songs that did end up on the album.

One of the several discarded compositions and song fragments recorded during the gestation of *Born to Run* was "Janey Needs a Shooter." A retooled version of it would appear on Warren Zevon's *Bad Luck Streak in Dancing School* in 1980.

There was still one last opportunity for Springsteen's prevarication and perfectionism to sabotage proceedings, and he almost took it. Following the album's completion, Jimmy Iovine turned up at the Baltimore hotel where the tour-bound Springsteen was then based to present him with the mastered recording. The artist played it on the low-standard equipment immediately available to him. After he did, he took it off his turntable, went to the window, and tossed it into the swimming pool below. He then began talking about issuing live performances, recorded at Greenwich Village venue the Bottom Line, instead.

We know, of course, that he was quickly persuaded of the insanity of such a course of action and duly yielded up to the label the album master tapes, but the incident serves as a perfect microcosm of the staccato, snaking, doubt-afflicted saga of getting *Born to Run* over the finishing line.

3 THE SCREEN DOOR SLAMS: SIDE ONE

THUNDER ROAD

Springsteen was a talented but initially somewhat undisciplined songwriter. For *Born to Run,* he deliberately jettisoned the verbosity of the lyrics of his first two albums. It was a maneuver that changed everything.

Born to Run starts in a rather peculiar way.

Few know more about the importance of sequencing than Bruce Springsteen; one of the reasons he is considered among the greatest live attractions in the history of music is the skill his setlists reveal in the art of juxtaposition and pacing.

How to explain, then, *Born to Run* commencing with "Thunder Road"?

By 1975, sequencing of albums was something of an art form. Where LPs tended to open explosively or at least emphatically—qualities usually associated with up-tempo songs—"Thunder Road" is an often mid-tempo, largely inconclusive, even meandering number. It's precisely the type of cut not considered the sort to get anyone hearing it for the first time sitting up in their seat with their appetite whetted for what might follow.

Not everyone considers *Born to Run* to be Springsteen's peak. For some fans, 1980's *The River* is his masterpiece.

Springsteen didn't invent class-based rock, but before *Born to Run*, examples of it were restricted to selected songs by the likes of the Kinks, Creedence Clearwater Revival, and the Rolling Stones.

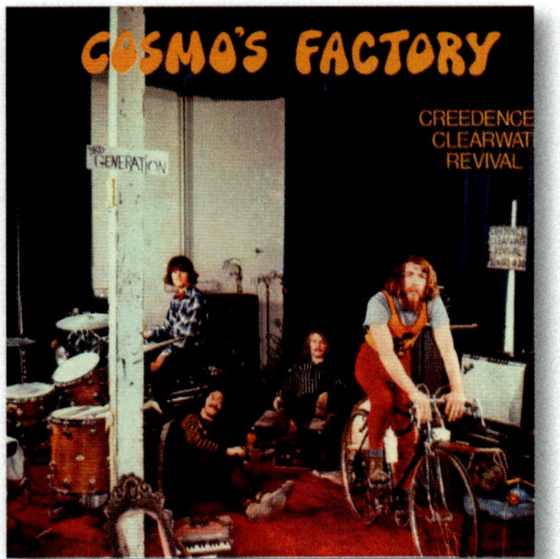

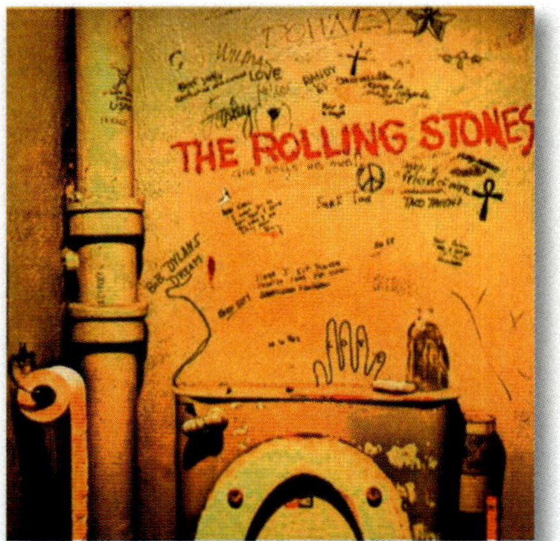

It has been suggested that Springsteen quite deliberately placed "Thunder Road" where it is because the song has the smack of an invitation to accompany the album's characters on the journey on which they are about to embark. However, Springsteen himself has said he made the decision to open with it over the towering "Born to Run"—which he admits would have "made sense"—because of the instrumentation. "'Thunder Road' was just so obviously an opening, due to its intro," he said to Brian Hiatt in 2005. "There is something about the melody that just suggests 'new day . . .'"

The song went under various guises, reportedly including "Wings for Wheels," "Angelina," and "Angelina's Dress Sways," before winding up as "Thunder Road." Its lyrics contain more than one example of future Springsteen trademarks. The first is popular-culture references. The very title is one, appropriated from a 1958 movie, although the song otherwise has nothing in common with that Robert Mitchum vehicle. It also famously contains a line about the narrator's beau's radio playing "Roy Orbison singing for the lonely." This reference to the Texas-born singer-songwriter's 1960 hit "Only the Lonely" is not gratuitous: It's delightfully followed by the observation, "Hey, that's me—and I want you only." The deployment of the reference is a mark of the fact that two decades after its appearance as what seemed the latest adolescent fad, rock now had its own internal mythos and an audience who had grown up steeped in its refrains and catchphrases.

The other soon-to-be emblematic element is discussion of motor vehicles in both literal and metaphorical senses. Turning up at the house of one Mary (whose "screen door slams" upon her appearance), the narrator persuades her that he's worth getting in his car for and then proceeds to take her down a highway that he insists is not just a stretch of road but a way by which the couple can escape this "town full of losers." It will not be the last time on this album—or by any means in his career—that Springsteen portrays a protagonist whose obsession with escaping his limited and constricting environment is illogically posited as having a symbiotic relationship with combustion-engine-assisted motion. However inchoate the symbolism, it can be rather stirring, especially when accompanied by music that not only supports but embellishes its pretensions: Hear how Springsteen advises Mary to "take hold" right before the tempo switches into a higher gear as if he's put his foot on the accelerator rather than just nodded at Weinberg to indicate that he should pick up the pace.

Some find such stuff laughable. This particularly applies to the UK, many of whose inhabitants always have had a problem with the very fact that Springsteen's poverty vignettes are so often speckled with automobile allusions: The idea that anybody can truly be said to be poor when they have the wherewithal for a set of wheels—even the second-rate

Springsteen has always deployed favorite phrases, motifs, and images; among them number wheels, escape, and women named Mary. They're all found in "Thunder Road."

type this song's reference to a "dirty hood" implies—doesn't have much traction in a country so fundamentally less rich than America, especially at that point in history. (That said, some of Springsteen's most fanatical fans can be found in Britain.)

The narrator alludes to a hoped-for sexual congress that he may well consider intertwined with his determination to "trade in these wings on some wheels." He also tells Mary, "You ain't a beauty but, hey, you're alright." Springsteen's narrator isn't just bluster, braggadocio, or boorishness—far from it. In "Thunder Road," Springsteen shows much vulnerability. He confesses to Mary his loneliness and virtually begs her not to turn him away on the grounds that "I just can't face myself alone again." He also says that he knows he's no hero. Popular music has always played host to male emotiveness, but singers begging their baby to come home or give them another chance is a tradition so mundane and stylized as to be devoid of the self-sacrifice involved in losing face by laying bare real emotion. The self-critical sensitivity of "Thunder Road" is rare for the macho mid-1970s. Springsteen's pioneering in this respect both here and elsewhere has to some extent been disguised by him being associated with loud, anthemic, and implicitly breast-beating music.

Structurally, "Thunder Road" serves as a microcosm of the track's unconventional placing. It possesses a sort of chorus, but the title phrase doesn't materialize until halfway through the proceedings and then doesn't appear again. It also boasts an instrumental break in the oddest place. After Springsteen had tried over and over to find an appropriate spot for Clemons to add his sax solo, he finally acquiesced to a suggestion by Landau to simply put it at the end to bring things to a conclusion.

All highly irregular, sure, but the fact that it's also highly effective is reinforced by the fact that "Thunder Road" remains one of Springsteen's most loved creations, regularly featuring near the top of fan polls of favorite Springsteen songs.

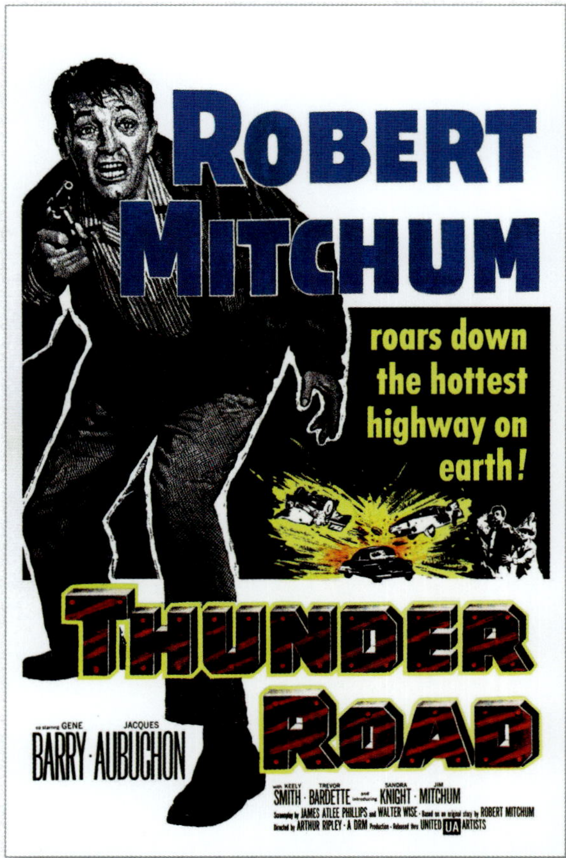

"Thunder Road" took its title from a 1956 Robert Mitchum thriller, but it's the only thing the movie and song share.

STEVEN VAN ZANDT

Springsteen's best friend since the pair's mid-teens was born in Massachusetts in 1950 but became a citizen of New Jersey at the age of seven. Van Zandt has been variously known as "Miami" Steve (because of his preference for balmier climes over New Jersey's variable weather) and "Little Steven" (which he adopted himself because his early idols included Little Anthony, Little Walter, and Little Richard). Following his days with Springsteen in Steel Mill and the Bruce Springsteen Band, he coled the band Southside Johnny and the Asbury Jukes.

While he didn't play on anything during the *Born to Run* sessions, the useful (if not often diplomatic) opinions and suggestions he ventured led Springsteen to formally make him part of the E Street aggregation upon the album's completion. Van Zandt made his stage debut at a concert on July 20, 1975. Starting with *Darkness on the Edge of Town* (1978), Springsteen gave him formal production credits.

Van Zandt was an important part of the E Street stage shtick, enabling Springsteen to dispense with axe work when the fancy took him. So much so that many were amazed when in 1984 Van Zandt left the E Street Band. Supposedly his reason was Springsteen's unwillingness to use the platform provided by success to engage in political campaigning work, specifically against the policies of President Ronald Reagan. Years later, however, Springsteen's semiofficial biographer Peter Ames Carlin made it sound like it was more about Van Zandt's frustration with an increasingly diminished production role.

Although he subsequently has returned to the E Street Band, Van Zandt has had a respectable recording career of his own, which has included leading the Disciples of Soul and organizing Artists United Against Apartheid. He has possibly become even more famous outside of the musical sphere, however, for his portrayal of Silvio Dante, a prominent fixture of the celebrated TV gangster drama *The Sopranos*. So celebrated was Van Zandt's portrayal of Silvio that he later reprised a similar role in *Lillyhammer,* a comedy series about an ex-mobster set in Norway, in which the Boss himself makes a guest appearance as a contract killer.

Steven Van Zandt has been best friends with Springsteen since the latter was fifteen. Here, "Little Steven" lays down a lick for his lifelong pal in 1983 at the US Festival in San Bernadino, California.

Van Zandt enjoyed a second career as an actor. He portrayed Silvio Dante on *The Sopranos* and later an ex-mobster in *Lillyhammer.*

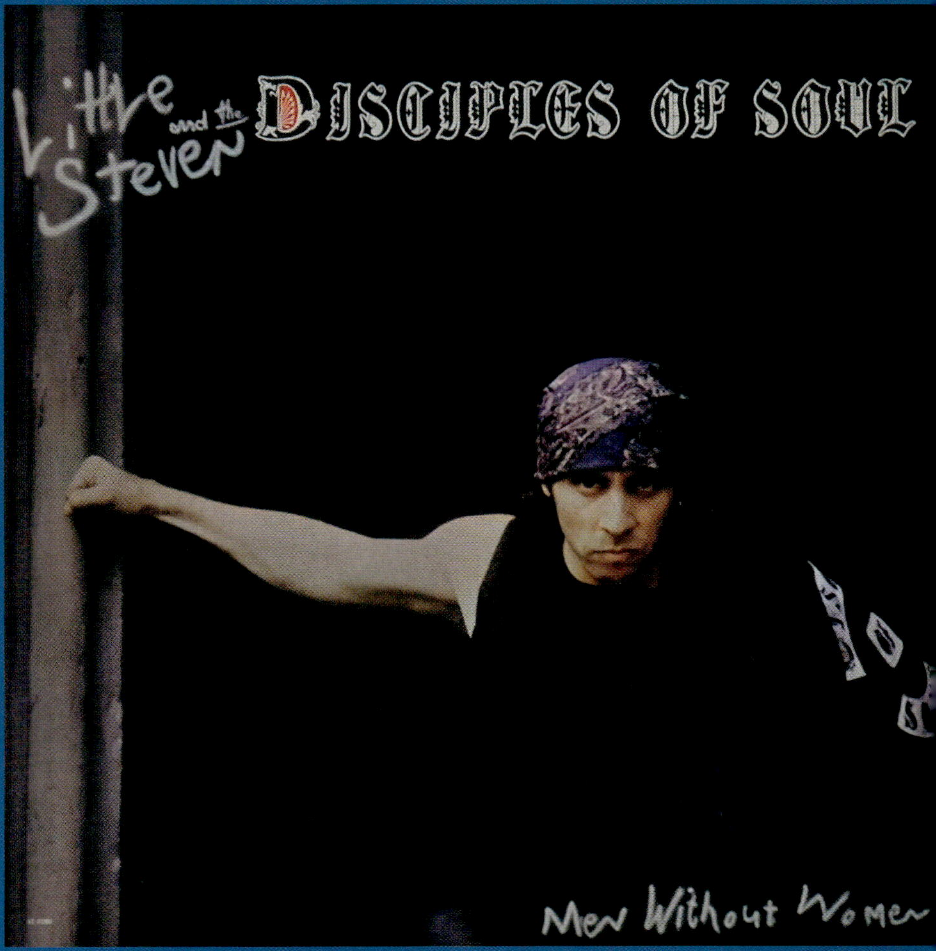

Van Zandt left the E Street Band in 1984 due to frustration over his diminishing role in production. Van Zandt's band Little Steven and the Disciples of Soul featured an uncredited Springsteen on backing vocals on their album *Men Without Women.*

Early idols such as Little Richard inspired Van Zandt's "Little Steven" moniker.

"Tenth Avenue Freeze-Out" is a rollicking number that captures the energy of New York City. It's also autobiographical. It features a character named Bad Scooter (i.e., Springsteen) who recalls the day the "big man joined the band" (i.e., Clarence Clemons).

TENTH AVENUE FREEZE-OUT

Musically, "Tenth Avenue Freeze-Out" is the bridge between *The Wild, the Innocent and the E Street Shuffle* and *Born to Run*. It's also in many ways the most likable cut on the album.

Partly this is because Springsteen's singing is delightfully syncopated as he belts out its elongated lines with a real rhythmic punch ("The night is *dark* but the sidewalk's *bright* and *lined* with the *light of the living*"). Partly it's down to the song possessing some of the record's most powerful sonics. The way the brass section blares out crisp and golden is a joy. It's fitting that Van Zandt should have first had an impact on Springsteen's recorded sound here, for this rock-soul hybrid purveys a biography of the E Street Band, albeit one that takes their story up to a point before he joined it.

Recording artists writing about themselves is often a dubious proposition at best and unwise at worst. The Rolling Stones' 1969 album *Let It Bleed* is often magnificent, but large swathes of it are dated by their insistence on playing up to their bad-boy image. Lines like, "I hope we're not too messianic/Or a trifle too satanic" are meaningless to subse-

MAX WEINBERG

Max Weinberg was born in Newark, New Jersey, in 1951 to a well-to-do family. His father was an attorney and his mother a physical education teacher.

He had been a drummer since the age of seven, but although he'd dabbled in playing professionally, he was in college and still living with his parents when he auditioned for the E Street Band vacancy in 1974. He is convinced he got the gig by never taking his eyes off Springsteen, enabling him to throw in accents and insert pauses appropriate to Springsteen performance. He has maintained that service-oriented approach ever since, a humility that is a stark contrast to his bellicose personality. Recording-wise, he came into his own on *The River* (1980), with the blazing style he employed on those sessions largely responsible for that album's barnstorming power.

Like the rest of his colleagues, he was devastated in 1989 when Springsteen disbanded the E Street Band to find out what working with other musicians was like. At one point, Weinberg contemplated abandoning music altogether, but he fell on his feet in 1993 when he was offered the job of bandleader on the Conan O'Brien nightly talk show, something that not only provided an income but made him more of a household name than he ever was while backing the Boss.

His session work alone could constitute an entire (and enviable) career for other drummers. Weinberg played on mega-sellers such as Meat Loaf's *Bat Out of Hell*, Bonnie Tyler's "Total Eclipse of the Heart," and Air Supply's "Making Love Out of Nothing at All." He also authored the excellent book *The Big Beat* (1984) in which he interviewed drumming heroes and colleagues like D. J. Fontana, Kenney Jones, Ringo Starr, and Charlie Watts.

From his earliest rehearsals with the E Street Band, Max Weinberg showed his attention to detail, which perfectly matched Springsteen's monomania about his sound.

quent generations to whom the Stones are merely a great group rather than the agents for social change they then represented. The Beatles' "The Ballad of John and Yoko" is an indubitably great track, but its central premise comparing John Lennon's tribulations at the hands of the media to Jesus Christ dying in agony on the cross is crass and offensive regardless of any religious convictions the listener might have. Autobiographical songs run like a seam through the Clash's entire catalog; "Garageland," "Clash City Rockers," "Last Gang in Town," "Four Horsemen," and "Radio Clash" are all enjoyable creations, but the way they posit the band as pivotal to music and culture is absurd when juxtaposed with the fact that the vast bulk of the general public had never heard of them.

"Tenth Avenue Freeze-Out" manages to sidestep any of these traps. For a start, Springsteen is way too nice and humble to engage in the big-I-ams of the Clash or the grandiose/grotesque overreach of Lennon, and he's not yet so prominent in the culture as to even think of portraying himself as totemic of values feared by anyone. He even manages to avoid coming across as self-indulgent. The listener is left thinking that songwriters write about themselves and their lives, and as Springsteen's life is that of a working musician, why not throw in a ditty about it?

e juxtaposition of Clemons's rtorial elegance and Spring- een's studied shabbiness s an amusing element of e E Street Band's mid-1970s age act.

As his esteem grew, Springsteen increasingly was sought out by public and press alike.

The song is not technically autobiography simply because it's not presented in the first person. The point of view is stated as being that of Bad Scooter, although it so happens Mr. Scooter shares initials with you-know-who. Recalling the day a "big man joined the band," the narrator doesn't state that said giant is 6 feet 4 four inches (193 cm) tall and the ensemble in question has "E Street" in its moniker, but he's clearly not talking about Charles Hawtrey and the Deaf Aids. Clemons's arrival is pinpointed as the moment the group was no longer vainly searching for their groove. The narrator then exults in the fact that the band proceeded to bust the city in half and that "little pretties" both there and all the way to the coastline began raising their hands, an assertion that would seem rather vainglorious were it not for the fact that—uneven and low-selling though his recorded output had been so far—Springsteen's reputation as a live act had indeed spread far and wide.

There seems some confusion-cum-deliberate ambiguity over the location of the titular street. References to the "city" seem to suggest that it is Manhattan's Tenth Avenue under discussion, a thoroughfare right down the block from where the vast bulk of *Born to Run* was recorded. However, there is also a Tenth Avenue in Belmar, New Jersey, one that happens to bisect the town's E Street that looms so large in Springsteen's life and lexicography.

More confusion surrounds the other part of the title. Being "frozen out" is a well-known, widely understood phrase meaning to be socially excluded, but Springsteen has admitted he has no idea what he meant by his use of "freeze-out" here. Most likely is that it was clumsy phraseology and a young man's love of cool-sounding wordplay—in contrast to the poised figure he presents today, the Springsteen of the 1970s was remarkably inarticulate, something of a stuttering, mumbling, leather-jacketed innocent.

GARRY TALLENT

The man who has been the E Street Band's bassist from its inception was not actually a native Jerseyite, having graduated there following his birth in Detroit in 1949 and an itinerant childhood. Nonetheless, he is deeply ingrained in E Street Band history, even to the extent of having graduated high school with Vini Lopez.

Learning the bass—and prioritizing it over the tuba, on which he also gained proficiency—Garry Tallent unashamedly cribbed from the best, including "Duck" Dunn, James Jamerson, Paul McCartney, and Bill Wyman. Despite having proven his bass-playing mettle by simple dint of being part of one of the planet's most renowned bands, he had sufficient humility to book lessons in the late 1970s with Atlantic R&B bass legend Jerry Jemmott.

Tallent once said of his bass playing, "Nobody notices I'm there until I'm not." Certainly you'd miss it if the conceptually appropriate throbbing lines he provides on the "Born to Run" track were absent. On other occasions, he actively improves already fine songs: Witness his lovely simpatico contribution to *The River*'s novelistic "Point Blank."

Relocating to Nashville after the E Street Band's temporary dissolution, he owned a recording studio, Moondog, and a music label, the D'Ville Record Group.

He never missed an E Street Band gig until the COVID-afflicted year of 2020. A combination of casualties and his long association with Springsteen means that Tallent is the E Street Band's only serving original member.

In this period rehearsal photo, Garry Tallent lurks behind Springsteen, lending credence to his quote, "Nobody notices I'm there until I'm not.

The phrase fits and makes sense, though, in that few people think about it. Those who do are too busy tapping their feetto care that it's not completely logical.

NIGHT

"Night" sees Springsteen adroitly capture the exhilaration of riding the nocturnal roads on two wheels. He describes in the second person the protagonist jockeying his motorbike through cars and waiting for the traffic lights to turn green, at which point, he notes, "With your faith in your machine/Off you scream . . . into the night" and we feel like we just left our stomach on the asphalt. The evocativeness doesn't stop there: "Every muscle in your body sings as the highway ignites" is the sort of stuff to make even non-riders want to clamber across a saddle and open the throttle.

Yet sadness lies behind the joy he portrays, demonstrated by the fact that the song begins far away from the joy associated with streetlight-dappled roads: "You get up every morning at the sound of the bell/You get to work late and the boss man's giving you hell." The narrator and his buddies are unskilled young people who can't wait for the end-of-day klaxon so that they can get home, grab a bite, and make their way to their vehicles. The glamour, power, and romance—hooking up with a beautiful young woman is stated to be a function of this activity—is all just a way of forgetting the fact that the daytime part of their waking hours is utterly gray and flat.

Springsteen's poverty in the period before the success of *Born to Run* was a difficult reality he had to deal with while waiting for commercial success.

Springsteen returned to this mordant-escape theme again and again in the next few years, and it's something with which some have a problem. By his own admission, Springsteen has never had a day job. This in no way ever excluded him from poverty. That scraping a living as a musician can lead to quite remarkable depths of penury and petty humiliation is illustrated by an anecdote from his autobiography in which he tells of his quest to pick up a paltry loan from Appel, which involved crossing a bridge with a toll payable in bills when he possessed only pennies. Springsteen, however, has enjoyed the good fortune to never have had to set his regular alarm for an ungodly hour and to never have had to spend the daytime performing tasks in which he has no interest or even hates. He has, of course, endured by proxy the consequences of low-wage unfulfillment: Endless stage monologues, interviews, and many pages of his autobiography have laid bare the frequent misery of growing up in a household whose head detests his son's existence due to his own lack of professional fulfillment. Yet there are some who feel

Clemons's saxophone was used to bring "Thunder Road" to a close after the production team found difficulty working out how to use it as a conventional instrumental centerpiece.

that there is an inauthenticity about his obsession with spiritual and financial poverty, an impression compounded in the mid-1970s by his then-preference for poetic phraseology over colloquial grittiness. Certainly, the interminable, relentlessly glum "Racing in the Streets" (1978)—similarly themed to "Night"—comes across as he-protesteth-too-much territory, leaving the listener feeling that, as Springsteen has managed to both move beyond his difficult childhood and escape the same fate as his father, he's hanging on to his historical grievances for purposes of professional victimhood. When all is said and done, though, it can't be denied that Springsteen knows whereof he speaks here on several levels. Nor that when he does speak, it's often with acute insight and power.

Musically, this track has less vigor than its lyric. Little wrong with the exciting opening drum salvo, Clemons's sinuous saxophone work, or Bittan's pounding piano. The fault lies in the fact that you can't hear them properly. The album's tilts at Wall of Sound grandiosity might be largely successful, but that production style often lacks sharpness because so many instruments playing at once necessarily means a tradeoff between power and clarity. Such clutter is not helped on this track by Springsteen's muffled singing of a lyric that is at least good enough to warrant a better delivery.

BACKSTREETS

Born to Run's briefest song ("Night" runs to 3:00) is followed by its second-longest.

The six-and-a-half-minute "Backstreets" begins with the most sophisticated musical passage of the album, the fulcrum of which is a glittering piano piece. This precedes a layering of organ redolent of Bob Dylan circa "Like a Rolling Stone"/"Positively Fourth Street." Springsteen makes his entrée in a somewhat less elegant way, his vocal harsh and sometimes indecipherable. The printed lyrics, however, show us that in the song he reminiscences, with eloquence and lyricism, about a lost relationship that took place against the backdrop of Nowheresville.

The fact that the narrator's ex-girlfriend is named Terry is part of a motif that is a source of amusement to Springsteen detractors and even some admirers. Just as much as the dreariness of working-class life and the joys of automobiles, it's a Springsteen keynote that almost every girl with whom his narrators become involved has a two-syllable first name ending in "y," whether it be Bobby, Candy, Cindy, Janey, Kitty, Rosie, Sandy, Sherry, Terry, Wendy, or—most commonly—Mary. (The rare likes of Rosalita must feel

The camaraderie of Springsteen and the E Street Band is evident in this stage shot of Springsteen, Clemons, and Van Zandt.

in a class of their own.) He may do it for reasons of meter or rhyme, but it comes across as lazy idealization: They sound more like movie characters than girls next door, and furthermore—to non-US ears—very cornball-American movie characters.

The narrator and Terry go back a long way to a youth in which they felt they could surmount their inauspicious surroundings by merely wishing for it. The narrator is now speaking from the perspective of disillusioned maturity, part of that disillusion stemming from the fact that Terry left him for another man, part of it from the way that life shatters convictions (remembering all the movies the couple would watch together, he recalls "trying to learn to walk like the heroes we thought we had to be"). Another passage sounds great in the tradition of song lines that veritably sing despite being opaque: "Tying faith between our teeth."

Elsewhere, though, Springsteen weakens his insight with hyperbole: "At night sometimes it seemed you could hear the whole damn city crying" seeks to make his perspective universal when of course many people in the city under question would simply not recognize or share his narrator's apocalyptical worldview. Another fault is that there's no getting around the fact that "Backstreets" would be substantially better were it a half-minute shorter. That doesn't mean thirty seconds should have been lopped off its back end, but Springsteen's interminable repetition of the title line in various degrees of emotiveness from roughly 4:50 to 5:55 could have comfortably been cut in half.

The assumption of most listeners that Terry is a female lover—bolstered by Springsteen using female pronouns in his various spoken-word preambles to stage versions of the song down the years—is called into question a little by a comment made in 1984 to British DJ and superfan Roger Scott. When Scott asked him about *Born in the U.S.A.*'s "No Surrender," Springsteen responded, "A song like that, or 'Backstreets' or 'Bobby Jean,' are just basic songs about friendship. . . . Me and Steve—we've been best friends since we were like sixteen, so anytime I wrote one of those, I had to be drawing on our relationship I guess to a certain degree. They're just songs about people passing through the rites of passage together." To be clear, this is not a statement that Springsteen swings both ways, but an acknowledgment or even admission that he habitually meshes romantic themes with friendship motifs. This is in fact symptomatic of a peculiar awkwardness in his writing: A man who isn't afraid to say he can't face himself alone is reticent about expressing affection for his male buddies, something that reaches a crescendo of gaucheness in the *Born in the U.S.A.* track "Bobby Jean," a farewell to the departing Van Zandt that he feels compelled to dress up as a goodbye to a girlfriend, one who for groan-inducing good measure has one of these all-American names ending in "y."

4

DOWN IN JUNGLELAND: SIDE TWO

BORN TO RUN

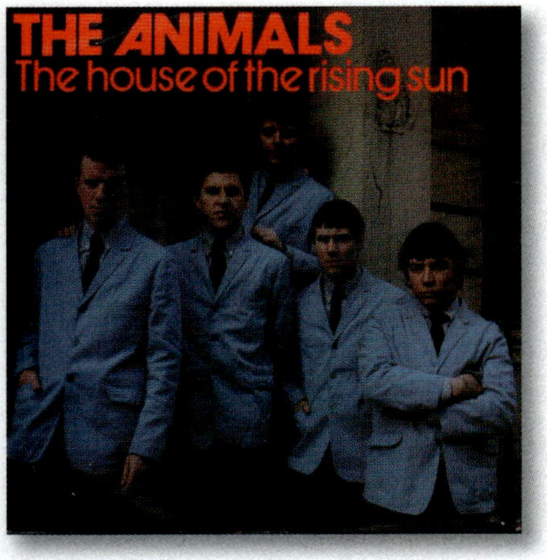

(Above) British 1960s R&B group the Animals were a major influence upon Springsteen, not least for their ostentatious proletarianism.

(Left) The second half of *Born to Run* opens with its full-throttled, open-throated, destined-for-immortality title track.

Born to Run may not be the greatest rock record ever heard, but what's not in dispute is the fact that "Born to Run"—a fist-pumping-anthem-cum-identity-asserting manifesto —remains the foremost among Bruce Springsteen's signature songs. Its symbiotic relationship with its creator and his image is only heightened by the fact that its title is a ready-made shorthand, ideal for Springsteen-related magazine-article headings and, of course, the composer's own autobiography.

The irony is that although it is rooted in intensely personal experience and feelings, "Born to Run" is really Springsteen's version of an Animals song. The UK quintet from the 1960s is most famous for its resplendent reimagining of folk standard "The House of the Rising Sun" (1964). The songs of theirs that spoke most strongly to Springsteen were a clutch of singles that—although none were written by any of the band's members —acutely captured their feelings about hailing from the underprivileged industrial north of England. The standard of living of the proletariat in the Animals' notoriously class-ridden homeland was then low, but that applied even more to their hometown of Newcastle. As such, they were able to invest real passion and belief in Mann-Weil's

The sight of the E Street Band onstage has always been a vista of vast talent.

"We've Gotta Get out of This Place," Atkins & D'Errico's "It's My Life," and blues traditional "Inside-Looking Out" (which may even justify Animals singer Eric Burdon and bassist Chas Chandler claiming part of the publishing of the latter, alongside blues archivists John & Alan Lomax). "To me, the Animals were a revelation," Springsteen later said. "The first records with full-blown class consciousness that I had ever heard." Springsteen would never be as great a singer as Burdon, but, whereas writing came quite hard to Burdon, Springsteen had the ability to compose his own class-conscious chorales when he pleased. "Born to Run" is the quintessence of those.

The introduction to "Born to Run" couldn't have made for a more stirring start to side two of the album's original vinyl configuration: a fusillade of drums, pulsating bass, a wall of saxophone, and Springsteen's reverberating seven-note guitar lick. The commotion soon gives way to a calmer, gently throbbing soundscape that provides the backing for a Springsteen vocal delivered in a solemn tone suitable for a statement that is, when it comes down to it, nigh suicidal. This despair is not immediately apparent because the narrator—addressing his girlfriend, Wendy—speaks of nighttimes spent riding through mansions of glory. Those mansions, though—as suggested by a first line that speaks of the American Dream in terms of an ever-receding mirage—are figures of speech, a metaphor for a snatching for solace.

Springsteen doesn't have a conventionally good voice but can be a master at conveying emotion.

We are back in the same psychological territory as "Night": The pleasure obtained from roaring down the backroads and highways constitutes the mansions in question; real mansions—or even decent homes—are and always will be nonexistent for the narrator's class of people. Unlike "Night," which is generally neutral, this track has an intimate, first-person perspective, thus granting it a greater impact.

Its narrator is acutely aware that his leisure-time activity is a form of self-delusion. The throbbing noise of his machine is ultimately bluster and smoke, and the motion he gives it—however high-speed—is ultimately a matter of going round in circles. He wants more, and he is all too conscious that he must lunge for it while he still has the urgency and capacity of youth. The people around him may share his view that his hometown—unnamed, but it's stated, just like Asbury Park, as possessing an amusement park, a beach, and a Highway (Route) 9—is a death trap/suicide rap/ripper of bones from backs. Unlike them, though, he insists that something can be done about it. What, though? Well, he isn't sure—he's simply determined to turn his engine-assisted motion from a leisure activity into a flight plan. *This thing moves, right?*, the logic goes. *Well, it's gotta take me somewhere, and somewhere else has gotta be better than here.* He thinks that somehow putting physical distance between himself and the trappings of home will, as if by magic, place him in different—i.e., better—financial and spiritual circumstances. In other words, this song is the *cri de cœur* of a loser who doesn't know he is one, which makes it all the more heart-rending when he vouchsafes to Wendy that he is convinced that "Someday, girl, I don't know when/We're gonna get to that place where we really wanna go and we'll walk in the sun."

For local boy Bruce Springsteen, Asbury Park's Highway 9/Route 9 looked good only when receding in the rearview mirror.

(Left) Reverse number? Springsteen's call of "One-two-three-four!" in "Born to Run" is up there with the Beatles' "I Saw Her Standing There" and the Clash's "White Riot" as one of the most famous count-ins in rock 'n' roll history—notwithstanding that it comes not at the beginning, as is traditional, but before the final verse.

(Right) Several of the characters in *Born to Run*'s songs are losers, of both "beautiful" and pathetic stripe. How ironic that with this album Springsteen proved that he himself was unequivocally a winner.

The song's chorus is a single-line lyrical refrain in which the narrator tells Wendy that tramps like them are born to run. The use of the word "tramp" is striking, even odd. He's using it to describe the low-born, and particularly the low-born who don't have the privilege of hailing from a vibrant metropolis with its greater access to employment, services, and diversions. "Tramp" is a word much more associated with poverty in the UK, where it's used to describe what Americans generally refer to as "hobos." Although Springsteen's deployment of it to mean the unwaged and uncouth is not unknown in his home country (witness the film *The Lady and the Tramp*), stateside it's more commonly a term for women of "loose morals."

That refrain inhabits the middle ground between the lyric's verisimilitude and its myth-making. The former is to be found in vignettes of boys trying to look hard, kids hanging aimlessly on the beach, and girls checking themselves out in the handy reflection afforded by rearview car mirrors. Cheek by jowl with such street-level reportage is heightened realism and poetic phraseology along the lines of that mansions-of-glory metaphor, whether it be the narrator's stated desire to die that night with his lips locked with Wendy's or the final-verse tableau of the highway being clogged with other locals trying to escape (which indicates that there are at least some others who share his ambitions). Springsteen also playfully throws in a verse where the desperation is leavened by ribaldry, the narrator channeling the innuendo of Benny Hill as he urges Wendy to wrap her legs around his velvet rims and strap her hands 'cross his engines. (This metaphor creates some ambiguity about whether the narrator is proposing escaping in a car—as many insist—or on a motorcycle.)

Max Weinberg was making contributions from day one of his tenure in the E Street Band: "She's the One" became a Diddleyesque shuffle at his suggestion.

Musically, that chugging scene-setting following the dramatic intro gives way to a sort of flowering, the music rising and opening out—abetted by a twinkling piano—as Springsteen describes young people roaring forth from Highway 9 in or on their dream machines. The pattern is repeated in verse two. An instrumental break sees Clemons's sax sally forth before we move into the bridge, an elegant piece of music befitting a switch into a less emotive, third-person perspective as Springsteen evokes the teenage revelries on a mist-shrouded New Jersey night. Perspective switches back to the first person for a passionate last verse directed at Wendy that ends in a dramatic "Huh!"; which serves as a starting pistol for a full unleashing of Springsteen's Spectorian ambitions. Multitracked instruments—including multiple guitar dubs—spiral to the sky as the music pounds and races. A respite follows before being broken by that classic rock 'n' roll count-in of "One-two-three-four!," one that presages the climactic final verse about the last-chance power drives that have snarled up the highway. A humming and whooing Springsteen takes the song to a clean, if exhausted, close.

Despite its quality, gravitas, eventual fame, and signature-song status, "Born to Run" was never a big hit. It made #17 on *Cash Box* and didn't even nudge into the *Billboard* top 20, stalling in the Hot 100 at #23. This was never a matter of import, and not just because this was the album-oriented 1970s; with "Born to Run," Springsteen had written a song that was several plateaus higher than anything to be found on his first two albums, and something clearly—finally—the work of a major artist rather than someone showing promise. It was—with utter irony considering its loserdom subject—the point when it was clear that Bruce Springsteen was destined for stardom.

Bo Diddley was a strong influence on *Born to Run*'s "She's the One."

SHE'S THE ONE

If the track "Born to Run" is Springsteen tilting for a Spector sound, "She's the One" is his take on the Bo Diddley style.

"She's the One" also marked Max Weinberg's first major contribution to the E Street Band. He had been in its ranks for only around a week when he suggested turning around the beat of a track that was currently cleaving to the rhythms of funk to instead take its cue from the Strangeloves' 1965 hit "I Want Candy," which was a nod to the hallmark of Diddley. Born Ellas McDaniel, Bo Diddley (1928–2008) was second only to Little Richard in lovable self-aggrandizement. That being the case, few were ever

DANNY FEDERICI

In *The River's* heartbreaking "Wreck on the Highway," Springsteen recounts the tale of a man who stumbles upon a road accident and who, as the ambulance he has called drives the fatally injured victim away, imagines a police officer calling on a wife to tell her the tragic news. Many will have been left without a dry eye as the ghostly organ Danny Federici contributes throughout fades away.

Roy Bittan's piano provides unobtrusive support on a track where Federici is dominant. Such give-and-take is the way the two men found to live with each other after Federici effectively boycotted the *Born to Run* sessions because he couldn't see where he fit into the Bittan-organized soundscapes. The accommodation of Federici doing his improv thang over and behind Bittan's tight arrangements gave the E Streeters (never otherwise particularly known for innovation) a unique sound.

Born in 1950 in New York but a man whose hometown was Flemington, New Jersey, Federici went back further with Springsteen as a bandmate than anyone else, having recruited Springsteen as singer for Child in 1969 and then worked with him for nearly two years in the renamed, evolving Steel Mill and again in Dr. Zoom. It was his turn to be recruited by Springsteen when Springsteen wanted an organist for his second album. Federici's nickname, "Phantom," was conferred by Springsteen when as a youth the organist laid low for a while after an altercation with the police at a gig.

Like his later E Street colleagues Bittan and Nils Lofgren, Federici was an adroit accordion player. He made a transition from that instrument to keyboards via the Cordovox, an accordion that could be turned on its side and played like an organ. His ten-year studies in classical accordion came to an end two weeks after he was properly introduced to blues and jazz. He contributed a fine accordion part in "4th of July, Asbury Park (Sandy)." His other instrument was glockenspiel.

The world lost Federici's talents far too early; in 2008, he succumbed to melanoma at the age of fifty-eight.

Few could, can, and possibly will ever sling an axe like Springsteen in his prime. Danny Federici can only look on in wonder.

inclined to argue the toss with him when he claimed, as he frequently did, to have invented the clave rhythm that provided the underpinning to many of his songs. What he insisted on calling the "Bo Diddley Beat" was a close cousin to both shave-and-a-haircut-two-bits and hambone. While he can't have been the first person to employ it, it *can* be said that he made it his own, creating a trademark sound in which the syncopated beat often took precedence over chord changes. On "She's the One," Springsteen co-opts Diddley's shuffling beat and shimmering ambience—surreally distorted instrumentation being another Bo hallmark—in a song in which he alternately exalts and denounces an object of desire.

That Springsteen is operating in a more permissive age than the one in which Diddley made his reputation is immediately apparent. "With her killer graces/And her secret places that no boy can fill" is about as bawdy as Springsteen gets. Unfortunately, he then proceeds to almost throw away his grand entrance by limping to the end of the first verse by rhyming that "fill" with "kills"—which isn't even a proper rhyme but then has "me" desperately appended to it. Considering that *Born to Run* is the archetypal work wrought of agonized perfectionism, it's astonishing that such sloppiness made it onto the record. Moreover, the lyric was once far more pointed, personal, and powerful than in the studio version—early renditions of "She's the One" found Springsteen talking of how much he hated his hometown and noting that the subject of the song was with him in New York at a particularly low ebb in his life.

Thankfully, he redeems himself after that lazy intro, even if the studio lyric never quite manages excellence. (A passage where he speaks of his subject's French cream and how it won't soften her boots any more than French kisses will melt her heart is the closest it gets to cleverness.) Moreover, the soundscape he marshals behind it is of a high quality. Bittan is the musical star of this cut, "trebling" up on piano, harpsichord, and organ, with his delicate work on the latter conferring a classy, tip-toeing leitmotif that contrasts with Springsteen's ultra-gruff vocal. Springsteen cuts across Bittan's delicate work with slashing downstrokes of electric guitar before the track gets fully into its disjointed groove. A soaring bridge provides a gateway to a Clemons solo that spurns mellifluousness and joins the overarching staccato spirit.

MEETING ACROSS THE RIVER

"Meeting Across the River" is more static geographically than the other material on the album. Yet it's also more layered and more of a true narrative than anything else on *Born to Run*, or in Springsteen's canon hitherto. Such story songs would now become part of Springsteen's repertoire. This one is the narrative of a real loser. That is, a true, nonglamorous loser.

Leonard Cohen's 1966 post-modern, surrealistic novel *Beautiful Losers* unleashed a monster. After Cohen coined the phrase, Bob Seger made it famous in 1975 with a song/album of the same name, helping turn it into a popular-culture leitmotif. The phrase was perceived by the wider public as articulating a feeling that had begun to grow since the 1950s: that being an unsuccessful—and often implicitly "wasted"—figure was as much to be admired as being a winner. It was in part a rejection of the conformism the Eisenhower era embedded in American culture and a reaction to the fact that so often in Western culture, success is associated with time-serving and blind obedience to rules. Simply put, a loser can be a tragic and glamorous figure if his lack of success can be framed in terms of a martyrdom based on a rejection of distasteful principles. The apotheosis of this inverted value system probably came when Finnish rock band Hanoi Rocks took the line "All those wasted years so close behind" from the Velvet Underground's desolate "Sunday Morning" and—clearly tickled to death that somebody had so acutely summarized their adoration of self-neglect, even if shot through with regret—turned it into an album title. *Born to Run* contains a lot of material in this vein. It didn't go down well with some people. In his (actually positive) review of the album, music critic Robert Christgau added the heavy caveat, "Springsteen needs to learn that . . . pseudo-tragic beautiful-loser fatalism insults us all."

Leonard Cohen—poet, writer, singer, musician. He coined the phrase "beautiful loser" in a 1966 novel. *Born to Run* was populated by characters who fit that description, to the delight of many but the disgust of some.

One of the reasons that Christgau's review was positive was because songs like the album's title track are—despite the way they mythologize and aggrandize self-pity—rather stirring. Although the protagonist of "Meeting Across the River" is no less a doomed outsider than the narrator of "Born to Run," "Meeting Across the River" isn't as rousing as "Born to Run," nor is it meant to be. Instead of a soaring anthem, we have music that is downbeat, melancholy, and even slightly dreary. We also have a narrative whose I'm-gonna-make-it assertiveness is not the forgivable self-delusion of someone who just wants to escape his surroundings but the whining, somewhat malicious self-justification of an individual who draws no distinction between petty rules and reasonable laws intended to protect the powerless and innocent.

ROY BITTAN

Opinions differ as to whether Roy Bittan (pronounced *Bitt*-en) was nicknamed "The Professor" by his colleagues because of his studious mien or simply because he was the only E Street Band member with a college degree. Either way, it feels appropriate to the educated timbre he brings to Springsteen recordings, one that often makes them feel like a musical category equidistant between rock and classical. His ornate style is particularly noticeable because few keyboardists who aren't leading their own band are as prominent in group soundscapes as Bittan is in Springsteen fare. His prominence on *Born to Run* is particularly appropriate because Springsteen, unusually, composed its contents on piano rather than guitar.

The E Street Band's first member with no connection to New Jersey, Bittan is a native New Yorker born in Queens in 1949. He attributes the expressiveness of his piano playing to the fact that his first musical instrument was the melodically evocative accordion. Before the E Street audition, he had played in bands and Broadway shows. He quickly confirmed beyond any doubt his importance to Springsteen's sound with his majestic contribution to "Jungleland" and has maintained that importance at crucial junctures. For instance, the synthesizer tones he contributed beginning with *Born in the U.S.A.* may not be to the tastes of inveterate rockers, but they helped keep Springsteen's sound contemporary in a changing musical landscape.

When Springsteen disbanded the E Streeters, it was only Bittan whom he retained. This was partly because of geographical proximity, but Bittan later became the first colleague with whom Springsteen formally cowrote songs, something that Springsteen has acknowledged helped him overcome writer's block. Not that Bittan would have been at a loose end otherwise: He has been employed as a sessioner by David Bowie, Jackson Browne, Bob Dylan, Dire Straits, Meat Loaf, Peter Gabriel, Stevie Nicks, Bob Seger, Bonnie Tyler, Bon Jovi, and Lucinda Williams.

Like the best virtuosos, Bittan combines the confidence in his own gifts that allow him to stretch out with a humility that enables him to rein it in. "A long, long time ago, I learned that the rests are as important as the notes," he once said.

(Left) Trumpeter Randy Brecker and (Right) stand-up bassist Richard Davis provided a mordant, noir ambience to "Meeting Across the River."

This individual is furthermore prepared to hurt people who get in his way as he sets about breaking such laws. Those whom it's clear he is prepared to harm to some degree or other include his long-suffering girlfriend Cherry—already aggrieved at him because "I took her radio and hocked it"—and the staff at the unspecified location at which it's clear he intends to mount a heist because he has heard two thousand dollars in cash is to be found there. The fact that he doesn't necessarily intend to use violence but merely its threat—Eddie, the pal to whom this entire monologue is addressed, is instructed to bulk out a pocket to make it look like he's "carrying a friend"—doesn't so much feel like mitigating circumstance as a mark of just how pathetically small-scale this man's villainy is. In short, this person is a loser even by losers' standards. Unlike in "Born to Run," where we can never be absolutely certain that Springsteen intends his narrator's unfocused thought processes to expose the hopelessness of his ambitions, this undermining is deliberate.

The conversational nature of the song words, and the ambivalent morality of the tableau they describe—one that can't be turned into the kind of allure that the roaring saddle-straddling and victimless self-delusion of "Born to Run" lends itself to—almost necessarily dictates that the accompanying music be a mordant matter purveyed only by piano (Bittan), trumpet (Randy Brecker), and stand-up bass (Richard Davis). (Springsteen is present only in the form of his vocal.) For all that, though, because the minimalist, jazzy setup with its echo-treated trumpet sounds like the soundtrack to a dozen dimly remembered film noirs, it ironically ends up conferring a certain neon-dappled beauty.

One layer of the song's psychology will have passed over the heads of those not conversant with the geopolitics of Springsteen's home state. Although never specified, the river in question is clearly the Hudson, which separates New York and New Jersey and demarcates the throbbing, sophisticated metropolis and the quiet, small-time backwater. There is an even further layer involved: Springsteen has admitted that when he

Springsteen's new lighting man Marc Brickman helped spread a buzz about the unrecorded "Jungleland" by giving it dramatic visual dimensions.

wrote the song, he was conscious of being at a low ebb career-wise, feeling like he'd been denied access to a citadel (i.e., commercial success, a big time in a way represented by New York) in which he felt he had a right to reside.

It's not just a deliberate lack of musical body that makes "Meeting Across the River" feel wispy and inconclusive. Another is the fact that at the close, the narrator and the listener are still no more certain than they were at the beginning that the desired jackpot-generating meeting is going to take place: we're left waiting for Eddie's answer to one of the interrogatives with which the narrator opened proceedings: "Can you catch us a ride?" That wispiness, though, is not in itself a fault, especially in the context of the *sturm und drang* by which the song is surrounded. In keeping with the idea of an album as a suite rather than a random collection of songs, "Meeting Across the River" is a vital piece of pacing, a respite, a quiet conversation between grand, bellowed pronouncements, the biggest and loudest one of which is about to follow.

JUNGLELAND

How to end an album like *Born to Run*?

With so much of it having been about grandiosity, the options included either subverting expectations with an understated finale ("Meeting Across the River" would have fulfilled that interesting option had Springsteen been so inclined) or going in completely the opposite direction of that with something grander than even the dramatics to which we have already been treated. Springsteen opted for the latter in "Jungleland."

It's a sprawling creation stretching to more than nine minutes whose music goes through multiple contrasting movements and moods and whose lyrics are pocked with incident and packed with larger-than-life but simultaneously low-rent characters. It comes across as a rock 'n' roll band proffering their version of a symphony or, yes, an opera.

Although it closes proceedings, in a sense *Born to Run* began with "Jungleland." Upon its live entrée, it had quickly become the highlight of Springsteen's stage act, with him exploiting the new dramatic possibilities afforded by his new lighting man Marc Brickman, using an overhead spot and a wider range of colors as he gave visual dimensions to his composition that included dying onstage. It whetted the appetite for Springsteen's long-awaited third long-playing release almost as much as the mix of "Born to Run" that had been leaked to friendly radio stations.

For some listeners, "Jungleland" has—and does—it all. A sweeping urban opus, it's peppered with girls on car hoods, boys" flashing guitars like switchblades," and cherry-top cops, and it is graced with a haunting saxophone solo.

"Jungleland" was reminiscent of *West Side Story* in its balletic, largely bloodless depiction of street life. Some found this admirable, some laughable.

Bob Geldof—seen here at a show with his band, the Boomtown Rats—was not a fan of *Born to Run*, dismissing "Jungleland" in particular as "fiction."

The only real fault in "Jungleland" is how vague and sprawling it is throughout its elongated runtime. Springsteen's lyric tries desperately to convey the idea that something of import—an outrage, in fact—has gone down, but in his insistence on opting for metaphor and poetry instead of plain-speaking reportage he never manages to clearly communicate what it is.

The action takes place one warm but rainy summer night somewhere in New York City, possibly Harlem, into which one Magic Rat has driven from his presumably native New Jersey. There he decides to romance a barefoot girl he meets sitting on a car hood. On the couple's trail, though, are local lawmen. The reason is unspecified, although it's implied that it's related to traditional police hostility toward young people assembling in groups at night. The "kids" on whom this composition focuses seem to be budding musicians and their entourages. By the song's end, it's suggested that the Magic Rat is deceased, shot by the local "cherry-tops" who have ripped "this holy night." Yet the lyric also states that "the Rat's own dream guns him down." This irritating opaqueness is compounded by the fact that Springsteen tends to drain the grit out of his street tableau by projecting an incongruous glamour, whether it be talk of a ballet being fought out in the alley, young people looking just like shadows, or kids flashing guitars like switchblades. The stylization and effete similes put one inescapably in mind of *West Side Story,* which, whatever its qualities, always felt like the Man's idea of street life.

"Jungleland" is the epitome of why some people can't stand Bruce Springsteen. For all the accolades and millions of sales he has generated, Springsteen leaves many discerning music lovers in the cold. The late and renowned British disc jockey John Peel dismissed his catalog on the grounds that it just "doesn't ring true." The Boomtown Rats' Bob Geldof once spoke of Springsteen with more vitriol, in the process quoting "Jungleland." "He's nowhere near as good as his hype," he asserted. "He writes fiction. The Magic Rat did not drive his sleek machine over the Jersey state line." Where others see grit and authenticity and an insight into a milieu often ignored not just by popular music but by arts and culture (especially in the 1970s), others just see phoniness. For them, the musical slickness of "Jungleland"—with its colorfully named characters, poetic phraseology, and balletic, bloodless incident—constitutes an almost comically milquetoast and blandly stylized portrait of the kind of world and mindset that can be represented only by linguistic and performative rawness.

Such criticisms may miss the point. Springsteen is the main progenitor of class-based rock (or what we must now call, in a world where rock is a small subgenre, Post-Presley Popular Music). As such, he had to devise his own rules for the path he chose to take his

Springsteen is the father of class-based rock, but the likes of the Sex Pistols and the Clash (below) proved that this new genre could take different forms. Some critics believed that punk made Springsteen's prototype seem risibly overblown and myth-laden.

music down. For all rock 'n' roll's libertarian and proletarian aura, it hadn't been terribly concerned with class until the mid-1970s. As Springsteen noted, one of the reasons he found the Animals' records so powerful is that their perspective from the bottom of society's ladder was lesser-spotted. Those and other examples of caste-consciousness such as the Kinks' "Dead End Street" (1966), Creedence Clearwater Revival's "Fortunate Sun" (1969), the Rolling Stones' "Salt of the Earth" (1968), Elvis Presley's "In the Ghetto" (1969), and the Small Faces' "Lazy Sunday" (1968) were rarities. They collectively formed altogether too small a sample to provide any kind of template. Perhaps it's natural that the boilerplate Springsteen invented for his new caste-aware bent starting with some of the tracks on *The Wild, the Innocent and the E Street Shuffle* was not the type of matter-of-fact documenting to be found in working-class literature like *The Grapes of Wrath* or *Saturday Night and Sunday Morning*, but instead the sort of approach to be found in motion pictures. Like the movies, music is a performative and by and large glamorous medium.

It was Springsteen's misfortune, though, that within two years of *Born to Run*'s release, the UK punk rock movement had comprehensively proven that class-based political songwriting could be rendered in a different way, one instantly recognizable as more logical. Part of punk's musical abrasiveness was its deliberate lack of technique, but even when the punks started acquiring competence on their instruments, they remained anchored by the naturalistic approach that their ground-level visions had been rendered in from day one. It turned out that colloquial, gritty lyrics set to glamorous sonic backdrops did not generate feelings of incongruity (cf. the Clash's *London Calling*, the Jam's *Setting Sons*). Had punk never come along and given people something with which to unfavorably compare Springsteen, he may be more highly regarded by Peel, Geldof, and other naysayers. Moreover, while punk served to make Springsteen's visions feel overblown and old-fashioned, without him it's difficult to imagine punk ever having come about at all. It is unquestionably Springsteen who paved the way for the likes of the Sex Pistols, the Clash, the Jam, Sham 69 et al., who may not all have been Springsteen fans but were given the opportunity by his catalog and success—most especially that of the *Born to Run* album—to proffer their own visions in the same terrain.

Moreover, Springsteen's poetic approach also has its attributes. The likes here of "The street's on fire in a real death waltz/Between what's flesh and what's fantasy" is stirringly expressive. Nor does the florid approach completely preclude verisimilitude; when he describes vignettes like a barefoot girl sitting on the hood of a Dodge, youths congregating beneath the glaring light of a giant Exxon sign—the more stylish amongst

Springsteen and Clemons were always a tight unit, but Clemons must have sometimes felt less than amiable toward Springsteen as he dictated to him the two-minute-plus sax solo in "Jungleland" note for note.

CLARENCE CLEMONS

The first encounter between Springsteen and the saxophonist who was for many years integral to his sound is one shrouded in myth or possibly baloney. Whether or not it was portentous that the doors of the Student Prince, the Asbury Park venue where they met in 1971, blew off their hinges that night is a matter of debate, but few doubt that they were instantly smitten with each other, to such an extent that their neglected respective girlfriends jocularly told them they were gay.

Clarence Clemens was born in 1942 to middle-class parents who worked as fish wholesalers. He was the not-too-grateful recipient of an alto saxophone from his father when he was nine. His admiration and aptitude for the instrument grew, however, on the chords and progressions of the masters of the instrument, particularly King Curtis, whose sax work famously graced records by the Coasters. He graduated from alto sax to baritone and ultimately tenor.

Besides Springsteen, Clemons worked with luminaries such as Aretha Franklin, Ringo Starr, Jackson Browne, Todd Rundgren, and Lady Gaga. He also became a successful film and television actor.

He died on June 18, 2011, following a stroke, leaving behind four sons from five marriages and the memory of a man whose larger-than-life personality perfectly matched his massive frame.

Clemons, Springsteen, and (hidden behind his drum set) Weinberg laying it down live. Even those who weren't partial to Springsteen's records couldn't deny the power of him and the E Street Band in the flesh.

them dressed in the latest rage—he paints a vivid picture of a subculture. He also proffers the type of snapshot of a moment in time that is rare because the window in which any artist is interested in documenting that moment closes so quickly: The crazes and ritualsthat make up the minutiae of youthculture are absolutely everything to teens and twentysomethings but matters of utter trivia, transience, and embarrassing youthful folly to anyone in their late twenties and beyond. The song is ultimately moving, especially Springsteen's climactic fury over the fact that the local scene's poets aren't interested in chronicling what they see around them until it's all too late.

Clarence Clemons's larger-than-life personality perfectly matched his massive frame. Though he's most well known for his work with the E Street Band, he also recorded with Aretha Franklin, Todd Rundgren, Lady Gaga, and more.

"Jungleland" possesses a seamless majesty in its structure and musicianship. It opens with *strings*. This and the other places they're faintly heard are the only remaining vestiges of the classical strains that the album was drenched in before Springsteen decided that they "kinda took away some of the darkness" and peeled them back. They thread this track in just the right proportions. Their sweet tone in the intro is intertwined with some particularly elegant Bittan piano work, after which an already breathless Springsteen begins his narration. His scene-setting builds in intensity as the tempo increases and other instruments join the fray, leading into a fine, greasy guitar solo. A switch of melody line presages a passage where Clemons is front and center with a twinkling, lengthy, pathos-drenched solo of more than two minutes. (Springsteen dictated it to him note for note.) This busy section subsides to find Bittan alone in the spotlight hitting melancholy chords, preparing the way for the narrator's relaying of the fact that the night's joyful events have ended in tragedy. Springsteen's mordant tone rises to a pitch of fury, the instrumentation matching him, as he denounces both the authorities and their victims. At the close—individual track and album—the overtone of a reprise of the classical strings is left hanging in the air to gently bring us down from a vast immersive experience.

5

BORN TO RULE: THE RECEPTION

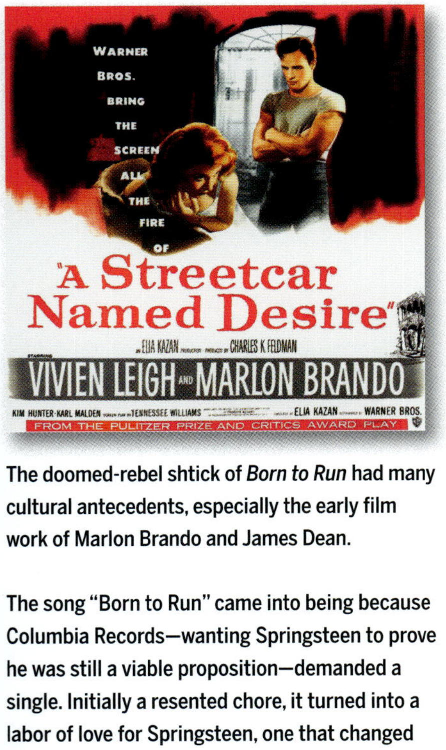

The doomed-rebel shtick of *Born to Run* had many cultural antecedents, especially the early film work of Marlon Brando and James Dean.

The song "Born to Run" came into being because Columbia Records—wanting Springsteen to prove he was still a viable proposition—demanded a single. Initially a resented chore, it turned into a labor of love for Springsteen, one that changed his entire approach to songwriting.

Born to Run was released on August 25, 1975, with a single featuring its title track backed with "Meeting Across the River" issued on the same day.

"Born to Run" was not immediately acclaimed as a classic. Mike Jahn of *High Fidelity* wrote, "To listen to a Bruce Springsteen record is like walking down Forty Second Street on a hot July afternoon," his review stated. "It's unusual, it's colorful, it's a little dangerous and interesting and out of the ordinary. However, one hesitates to take the journey twice." While he acknowledged that any pop composer who attempts to say more than "I love you" or "Let's dance" should be encouraged, he found Springsteen guilty of considerable repetition: "He has created a host of contemporary Damon Runyon figures but, in the course of three LPs, has said more than needs to be said about them." He found some merit in the title song ("a semi literary version of Steppenwolf's 'Born to be Wild'"), "Thunder Road," and "Meeting Across the River," but his conclusion, in which he invoked the main male character in the stage classic *A Streetcar Named Desire*, was, "It's heartening to recognize the existence of a rock composer thoughtful enough to want to create his own Stanley Kowalski. Now if Bruce Springsteen were only Tennessee Williams he might produce rock works of true and varied literary value. But he isn't."

Some critics were distinctly unimpressed by Springsteen. Langdon Winner described him as someone threatening to become "the consummate bore" while Roy Carr accused him of "purveying Surreal Nostalgia at near-psychotic levels."

The Real Paper did not seek to dictate that any review should follow the orgasmic Jon Landau line about Springsteen's merits. Langdon Winner—an esteemed critic probably most famous for adjudging the Beatles' *Sgt. Pepper's Lonely Hearts Club Band* a "decisive moment in the history of Western civilization"—was utterly underwhelmed by what he heard. He sneered that Springsteen "has gone to the finest pop schools. He respects his elders. He bears the finest credentials and upholds the highest standards. Like all dutiful epigone, he threatens to become the consummate bore." *Born to Run*, he said, was "the complete monument to rock and roll orthodoxy." His perceiving demerit in Springsteen's penchant for acknowledging and echoing pop landmarks was in some ways prescient of the topple-your-idols credo of punk, but it was Springsteen's very love of rock that other critics found attractive.

Rolling Stone gave the task of reviewing the album to veteran rock critic Greil Marcus. He proved a judge just as sober as Jahn, though ultimately more impressed. He noted, "With two 'you gotta see him live' albums behind him, the question of whether Springsteen would ever make his mark on rock & roll—or hang onto the chance to do so—rested on that third LP." Marcus found Springsteen's answer in the form of *Born to Run* to be "a magnificent album that pays off on every bet ever placed on him." He invoked the entire now two-decade-old history of rock and the counterculture in stating, "Springsteen's singing, his words and the band's music have turned the dreams and failures two generations have dropped along the road into an epic—an epic that began when that car went over the cliff in *Rebel Without a Cause*." He said the album was composed of "tales of kids born to run who lose anyway" and asserted that "the songs can, as with 'Backstreets,' hit so hard and fast that it is almost impossible to sit through them without weeping,"

Greil Marcus, seen here in 1982, was assigned by *Rolling Stone* the task of assessing *Born to Run*. Marcus hailed it as "a magnificent album that pays off on every bet ever placed on him."

Not least of the reasons for Greil Marcus's admiration for *Born to Run* was that he saw it as plugged into the rebel mindset. It picked up the cultural touchstone that went back to the moment "when that car went over the cliff in *Rebel Without a Cause*."

adding, "And yet the music is exhilarating." Proving he was as adept a reviewer as Jon Landau in coming up with a memorable phrase, Marcus described the record's sound as "a '57 Chevy running on melted down Crystals records."

Robert Christgau specialized in capsule album reviews graded using schoolteacher methodology. His *Village Voice* summary started unpromisingly ("Just how much American myth can be crammed into one song, or a dozen, about asking your girl to come take a ride?") and was, as noted previously, scathing about the beautiful-loser mythology Springsteen embraced. He also had problems with the album's "operettic pomposity." However, he had to concede that usually Springsteen avoided or simply ran over such quibbles: "If 'She's the One' fails the memory of Phil Spector's innocent grandeur, well, the title cut is the fulfillment of everything 'Be My Baby' was about and lots more." He awarded the album an "A" grade, which the key to his grading system defined as "A great record both of whose sides offer enduring pleasure and surprise. You should own it." According to his own estimate, only twelve to fifteen albums of "A" quality were released in any given year.

Upon first glance, critic Robert Christgau (foreground) was not impressed with *Born to Run*'s mythologizing of the working-class loser. However, the review ultimately conceded that Springsteen's third album was a great work.

For more than a decade preceding *Born to Run*, rock had been all but owned by British artists. With Springsteen, US critics and fans finally had a homegrown artist who could hold his own with the likes of Led Zeppelin and the Rolling Stones.

The *New York Times*' John Rockwell opened with a familiar motif when he observed, "The trouble with Mr. Springsteen's career . . . is that his records haven't matched the astonishing impact of his live performances." Of his third LP, he wrote, "The range is as wide as either of the earlier albums, from poignancy to street-strutting cockiness to punk poetry to quasi-Broadway to surging rock anthems. But all of it (except 'Meeting Across the River,' which works superbly on its own terms) is solidly rock 'n' roll." While he claimed, "Sometimes his lyrics still lapse too close to self-conscious myth making," he also found them "overflowing with pungent detail and evocative metaphors." Like many, he also found Springsteen's themes to evoke not just specific incidents but rock culture per se, being full of "cars and love, street macho and desperate aspiration." He asserted that hearing these songs was like "hearing your own life in music." He concluded that "*Born to Run* seems one of the great records of recent years. . . .You owe it to yourself to buy this record."

Creem's Lester Bangs was a critic destined to shortly fall in love with punk rock. He was also not easily impressed. Nonetheless, Bangs took completely the opposite point of view to Winner. While he condemned critics "making extravagant claims for him, backed up by one of the biggest hypes in recent memory," he asserted that "*Born to Run* will probably be the finest record released this year." He also said, "If I seem to OD on superlatives, it's only because *Born to Run* demands them."

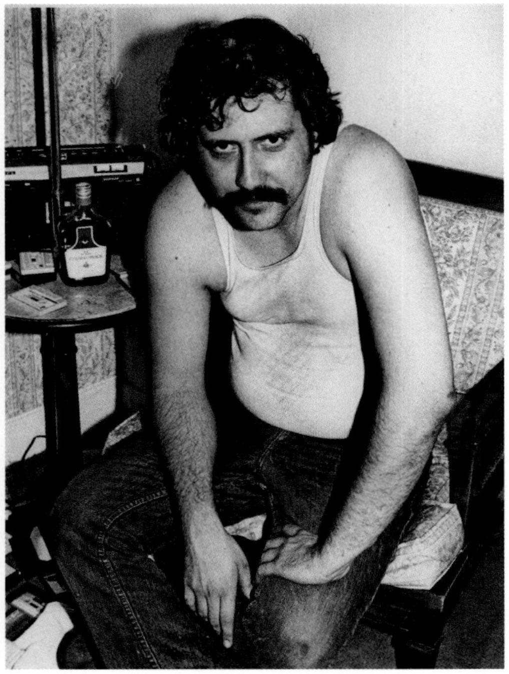

In the mid-1970s, critic and *Creem* editor Lester Bangs was increasingly disenchanted with rock music. He saw *Born to Run* as an antidote to what he saw as its artistic ossification and increasing sociopolitical irrelevance. "If I seem to OD on superlatives," he wrote, "it's only because *Born to Run* demands them."

Significantly, another line in Bangs's review found him celebrating *Born to Run* for being "an American moment caught at last." It's not a slight on Springsteen or the critics who lauded *Born to Run* to say that one of the reasons the album was so loved by so many American critics must surely be patriotism. It was the United States that invented rock 'n' roll, but since the early 1960s the UK had owned it. With a few exceptions like Bob Dylan and Jimi Hendrix, the most important artists since then—from the Beatles to the Rolling Stones to the Kinks to the Who to Led Zeppelin—had been British acts. (The Beach Boys, of course, don't count because they slightly preceded the Beatles.) Finally, Americans had an indigenous rock talent fit to stand in the pantheon alongside those artists.

British critics had no such nationalistic feelings invested in the artist. They were also harder to please. Moreover, the contributors to the British music titles—*New Musical Express, Melody Maker, Record Mirror,* and *Sounds*, all large-format weeklies produced on newsprint—had, like the greater British nation, a less reverent approach to artists and celebrities in general. (British newspaper reviews were not going to be part of the *Born to Run* equation much—no paper at the time took popular music seriously enough to cover it properly.)

"Just how much American myth can be crammed into one song, or a dozen, about asking your girl to come take a ride?" wryly noted Robert Christgau in his actually positive review of *Born to Run*.

(Right) Regardless of the disdain of some critics, *Born to Run* sold and continued to sell, while the album has long entered the ranks of acknowledged classics.

It could be said that the true test of *Born to Run* would be how the Brits reacted to it when it was released there on October 10. (Some UK reviews ran in September courtesy of either imports or "white label" promotional copies.) Sure enough, they proved less liable to gush than their stateside cousins. However, the skepticism of Jerry Gilbert of *Sounds* was at least not gratuitous, being based on deep knowledge of Springsteen as both recording artist and live act. He was unimpressed by the recalibrated E Street Band. "There was a special charge about that voluminous yet incongruous bunch of New Jersey bar musicians that were the old backing band," he bemoaned. He said of Springsteen's new sound that it "for the most part is tight R&B" rather than the "stretched out episodic street-life ballads" that characterized *The Wild, the Innocent and the E Street Shuffle*. He lamented, "The metaphor is still vibrant in Springsteen's tales of seedy back-alley associations, but the vocal is often muted and brought back into the ensemble leaving no room for the extended monotone or near monologue through which Springsteen unwound his earlier tales." While finding "Night," "Jungleland," and "Meeting Across the River" all "a model of structure composition," he said that elsewhere "the band fails to convey the variation of mood that Springsteen's songs demand." He reserved particular criticism for the overly urgent production style of Appel and Landau, who he opined "aren't able to provide the necessary dispassionate ears to detect studio foibles" (coproducer Springsteen for some reason not being held partly accountable).

Columbia may have been accused of hyping Springsteen, but even they weren't anticipating the sales levels of *Born to Run*. His label authorized a domestic press run of 175,000 copies, but advance retail orders were 350,000.

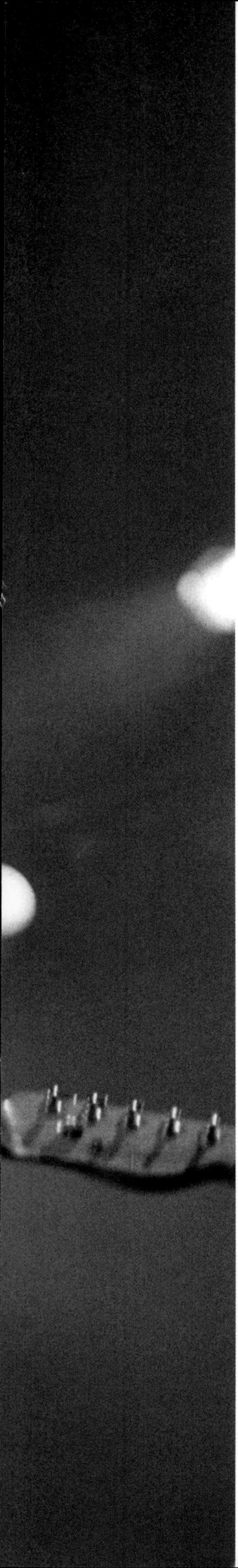

He concluded his connoisseur's evaluation of Springsteen's latest effort by saying, "This is not an essential album to have in the way that the previous two were" and explained that it was partly because Springsteen's brilliance was "now contained rather than allowed to run free." In summation, he said of *Born to Run*, "I have grown to love it but newcomers to Springsteen's music would be better advised to check out what the critics have been raving about in the past. Old fans will need to persevere."

Roy Carr of the *New Musical Express*, on the other hand, approached the album from the point of view of a man who had never been particularly enamored of the Boss at all. As Carr was the closest thing to royalty British rock criticism had, his opinions carried some weight. "Unlike critic Jon Landau, I've not been blessed with a vision of Rock 'n' Roll's Future etched in flames on a tablet of stone—but one thing that I *do* know is it won't answer to the name of Springsteen," he began. For him, "Springsteen isn't an original, but an extremely astute—though not greatly inspired—*ideas man* . . . with an angle on purveying Surreal Nostalgia at near-psychotic levels."

His contempt for what he perceived as Springsteen's pandering, stylized, secondhand shtick was supreme. "His skillful portrayal of the stereotype guitar-slinging street-corner punk (just outside the law—but not so he'll get trashed) is so well-defined that Hollywood couldn't have cast the role more accurately." Springsteen was only "moderately talented," with melodies, riffs, rhythms, and hooks that sounded "as if they floated straight off the car radio and into Springsteen's subconscious," and "he often tries too hard, going right over the top on many occasions as a result." Furthermore, the album's lyrics gave "themselves away with their studied elegance" whose "consciousness is strictly confined to *West Side Story*." Although the instrumentation was "reasonably dynamic," it got "less profound with each successive play."

Whether related or not to the doubtful scrutiny of the country's music press, *Born to Run* was notably less successful in the UK than stateside, making it only so far as #36 in the album chart in 1975 and not entering its top 20 until 1985.

Not only was the reception to *Born to Run* a mixed one, but the Springsteen gainsayers would shortly become increasingly vocal. As some of the review quotes indicate, the gargantuan $250,000 Columbia put into promoting *Born to Run*—itself a self-aware attempt at a new American masterpiece—created something of a backlash. Talk began gathering of the Springsteen hype. Only five years after the end of the intensely right-on 1960s, hostility to hyperbole was still quite prevalent, and rock consumers—whose preferred music was inextricably bound up with anti-corporatism—were the most vociferous of those inclined to denounce ballyhoo backed by big business.

THE ART AND PACKAGING: WRAPAROUND REVELRY

The impact of great albums is not necessarily dependent upon them arriving in great covers. There is, however, a pleasing symmetry about an album whose graphics live up to its sonics. *Born to Run*'s dramatic imagery across its gatefold sleeve is emblematic of the album's vivid and widescreen nature.

This appears to have occurred more through serendipity than calculation. On June 20, 1975, Springsteen stepped foot into the photography studio of Eric Meola, a snapper on the cusp of his thirties with whom he'd already made an acquaintance. Springsteen had only a vague idea of a picture that would feature both him and Clarence Clemons, who accompanied him to the shoot. Springsteen decided he wanted to represent their bond, although it seems safe to assume that he also wished to communicate something about racial relations. "Instinctively, I knew there was something about the two of us standing side by side that I wanted to say," Springsteen wrote in his *Born to Run* book. Springsteen arrived to the session in a ripped T-shirt and jeans, augmenting the outfit with a newsboy cap, an Elvis NYC Fan Club badge, and a transistor radio. Outtakes from the two-hour photo session variously show the pair back-to-back, Clemons lifting Springsteen, and a bare-chested Clemons flexing his biceps while Springsteen looks noncommittal. There are also multiple shots where one or the other is yawning—a manifestation of the fact that they were still working long days on *Born to Run*.

The image finally selected features a bent-kneed, fedora-sporting Clemons pretending to blow on his sax while a leather-jacketed, Telecaster-wielding, capless Springsteen leans chummily on the shoulder. (Out of shot is the 4-inch [10 cm] box Springsteen had to stand on to appear the same height as his buddy.) There were around seventeen similar frames, but the choice was limited insofar as in only two of them does Springsteen have his face turned toward Clemons and in only one of them is Springsteen grinning. The picture could have been reproduced in a smaller size on the front cover—as indeed it was on the picture sleeve of the "Born to Run" single—although it might have created confusion among the uninitiated as to why the billed artist was accompanied by another person, or even which of them *was* the billed artist. Perhaps it was this that motivated Columbia's art director John Berg to suggest that it lap the back cover. Turning the sleeve into a gatefold affair created a new dimension of interactivity, as the picture could then be completed and seen by opening the jacket. Gatefolds were usually only employed for double albums, and Springsteen was granted special dispensation to feature a gatefold for this single set.

The result was immediately intriguing. Springsteen dominates the front cover, but it's clear that there's someone else in the picture. Flipping the jacket over shows Clemons situated beside the album track listing and musician credits. Opening the gatefold gives the whole picture, albeit with part of Clemons scrunched up by the LP spine.

Despite the inherently deluxe nature of a gatefold sleeve, there is a minimalism to the album's design. The photograph is black and white. The lettering—although in a classy font and unusually detailed in its meticulous listing of the contributors—is set against a pure white background. (The first pressing of the album featured the artist credit and title in a faux hand scrawl. It was arguably conceptually more appropriate, but Springsteen preferred a tidy, formal look and had it changed, thus leading to an instant collectable.)

Inside the sleeve, a small pic of a smiling Springsteen running his hand through his hair sits atop a double spread of the album's lyrics, which Springsteen had included because he'd received many letters from fans complaining about their absence on the previous album.

The sleeve was much parodied: first on Cheap Trick's *Next Position Please* (1983), and subsequently on Tom and Ray Magliozzi's *Car Talk: Born Not to Run* (2003), female Japanese singer-songwriter's Mai Kuraki's single "Stand Up" (2001), and—perhaps most memorably—*Sesame Street's Born to Add* (1983), on which Bert took the role of Springsteen and the Cookie Monster stepped into the sax-blowing shoes of Clarence Clemons.

All the imitation merely underscored one fact: how distinctive, inviting, and timeless the *Born to Run* cover design was.

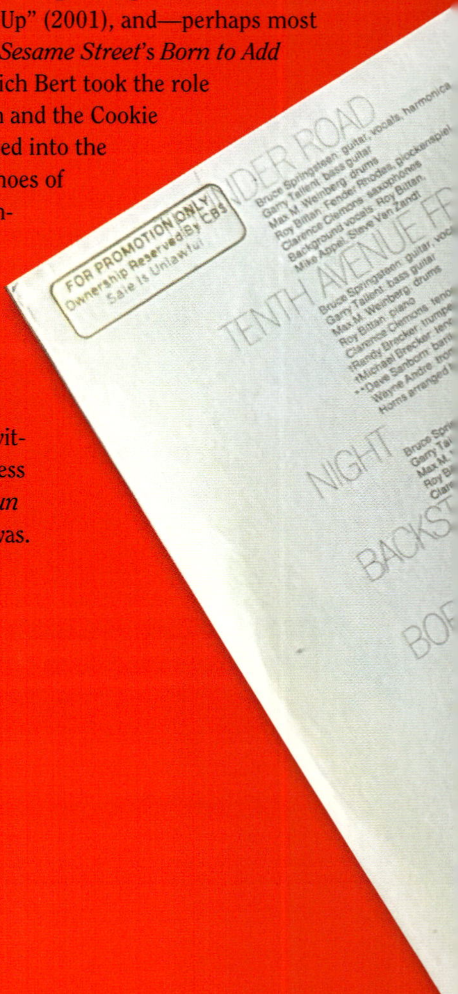

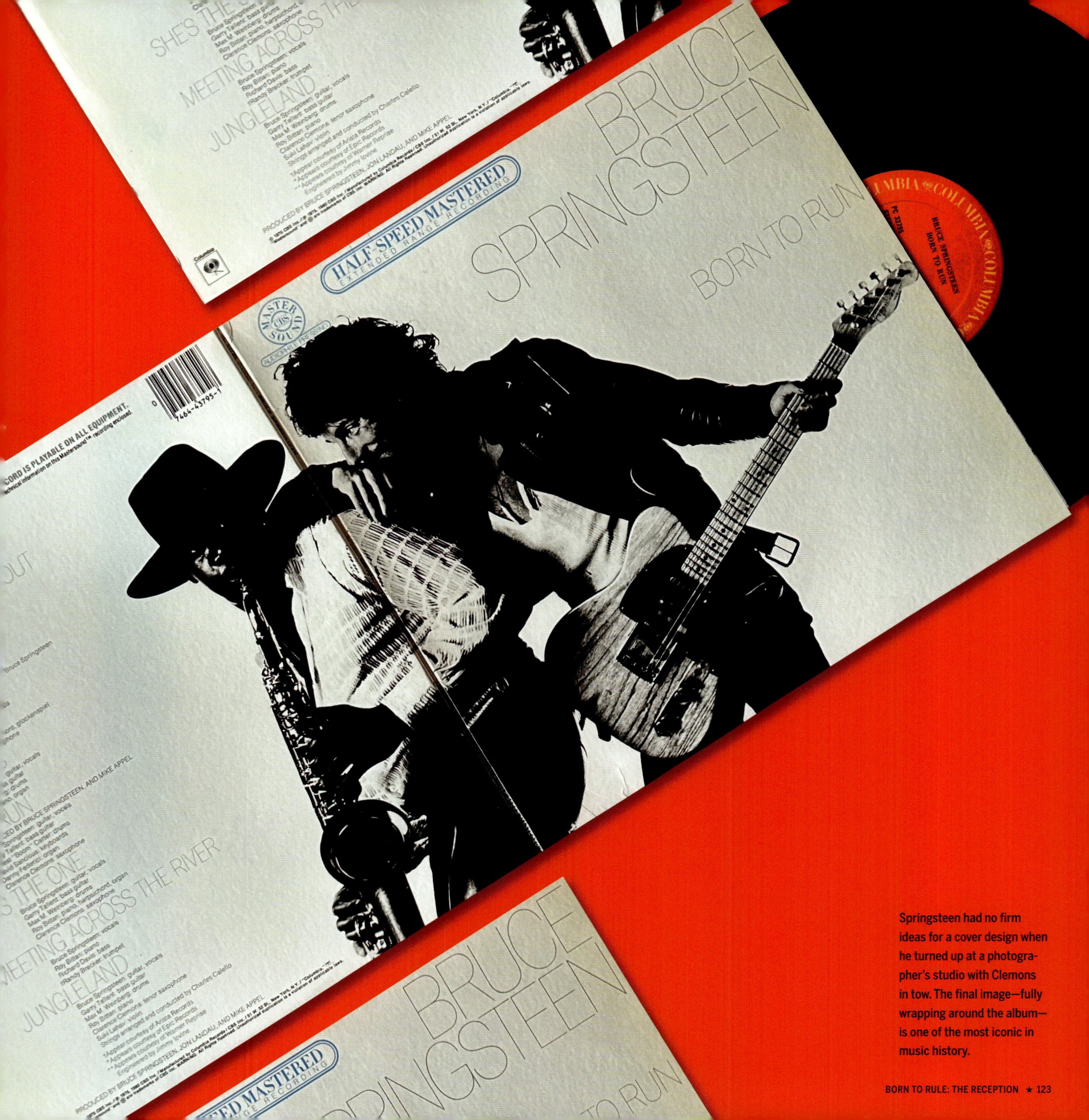

Springsteen had no firm ideas for a cover design when he turned up at a photographer's studio with Clemons in tow. The final image—fully wrapping around the album—is one of the most iconic in music history.

The *Born to Run* tour had a couple of odd additional legs. The reason that Springsteen was still touring in 1976 despite having no new product to sell was a legal dispute with manager Mike Appel that had frozen his record royalties.

But did any of the criticism have any effect? We'll never know. What we do know is that Columbia initially authorized a domestic press run of 175,000 copies, a wholly inadequate sum in the face of 350,000 advance retail orders. By the time it had been in the stores two months, *Born to Run* had shifted 700,000 copies, well on its way to racking up the nice, round, and lofty figure of one million. Until this point, that would have qualified it for a gold record, but the year after *Born to Run*'s release came the introduction by the Recording Industry Association of America of the platinum record (one million album sales or two million single sales). At the time of this writing, *Born to Run* has racked up approximately eight million documented sales (with the caveat that many more copied or downloaded Born to Run albums push that number unquantifiably higher).

Sales often signify nothing about either a work's artistic worth or its capacity for longevity in public affection. For example, only half a decade after they straddled the globe like colossi, it was difficult to find anyone prepared to admit to ever loving Emerson, Lake & Palmer, Humble Pie, or the Knack. The reputations of these bands (and many more before and after them) all swung back around in the court of public opinion, but for millions of people, a what-did-we-ever-see-in-them? aura will always hang over them. *Born to Run* is one of those albums, however, whose standing has been confirmed, even enhanced, by the passing decades. In 1978, three years after its release, it came tenth in a book-length poll conducted by BBC DJ Paul Gambaccini among music critics and industry figures to determine the greatest albums of all time. When "Gambo" repeated the exercise nine years later, it had risen to second place. It consistently makes the upper echelons of *Rolling Stone*'s regularly revised 500 Greatest Albums of All Time poll, even though some might assert that the pundits chosen to compile it have been altered in a deliberate attempt to "correct" the prominence of white, male musicians in early versions. In 2004, *Born to Run* was listed in the Library of Congress's National Recording Registry of "culturally, historically, or aesthetically significant" recordings.

Springsteen's early Bohemian look gave way post–*Born to Run* to a clean-shaven and more stylish appearance.

In other words, it has long been clear that it's an album born to run and run and run.

THE *TIME-NEWSWEEK* DOUBLE WHAMMY

In 1975, the weekly news magazines *Time* and *Newsweek* were the main national sources of information for millions of Americans.

Some musical artists such as Joan Baez and the Beatles made their covers in the 1960s, but at that stage, the perspectives of *Time* (founded in 1923) and *Newsweek* (which made its debut ten years later) were then still a little beholden to old-order shibboleths such as that low culture cannot really be considered great art.

By the mid-1970s men working in offices, including those of *Time* and *Newsweek*, might still be wearing neckties, but some of them had longer hair than that with which the Rolling Stones had outraged large sections of society ten years earlier. A new generational influx was bound to have an effect on notions of journalistic values. Cher and Elton John had already made the cover of *Time* in 1975. On the edition cover-dated Monday, October 27, 1975—just shy of two months after *Born to Run*'s release and it so happens Mike Appel's birthday—they were joined by Bruce Springsteen. Astonishingly, Springsteen—an artist without a hit song to his name and still playing clubs—also made the cover of the same week's edition of *Newsweek*.

Appel had done it again, engineering a coup as big as the Hammond audition. When media outlets, alerted to the supposed hot new thing by Columbia's advertising department's spending spree, contacted him about the possibility of an interview, Appel put on his hustler's hat. If they wanted Springsteen to speak to one of their reporters, they had to promise that the artist would feature on the front cover of the relevant edition. One might imagine that it took some chutzpah to thus jeopardize coverage in periodicals with such titanic circulations (*Time*'s was 4.25 million, *Newsweek*'s 2.9 million). Yet somehow he bent the editors to his will.

The first to buckle was *Newsweek*, although some have read Machiavellian and retributive motives on its part. The September 8 edition had included a short piece on Springsteen with a tart note about how Appel had banned interviews if they weren't cover stories. *Newsweek*'s senior editor, Lynn Young, had an idea about a feature on the making—which seems to be a code for "cynical manufacturing"—of a rock star. With accusations of Springsteen hype beginning to snowball, she had decided that the New Jersey boy was the ideal subject. The coverage of Springsteen in America's premier news magazines might have well been restricted to this potential hatchet job were it not for the fierce competition between the two periodicals. Jay Cocks, *Time*'s film critic, was a Springsteen fan. After hearing of *Newsweek*'s intentions, he successfully petitioned the editorial staff to run a story on him.

The *Time* cover featured a head-and-shoulders illustration of a bare-chested, newsboy-cap-wearing Springsteen wielding a guitar and a mile-wide grin. Inside, Cocks's write-up—from interviews conducted by colleagues—was titled "The Backstreet Phantom of Rock." Quoting liberally and admiringly from Springsteen's lyrics, it was as laudatory as one might imagine

The man declared by the cover of *Time* to be "Rock's New Sensation" seems to channel an older one—Pete Townshend—while onstage in Amsterdam.

from the cover strapline "Rock's New Sensation." He had the integrity to acknowledge that Springsteen was less rock 'n' roll's future than its past ("Springsteen has taken rock forward by taking it back, keeping it young. He uses and embellishes the myths of the '50s pop culture"). After admitting that Springsteen "does not smoke, scarcely drinks and disdains every kind of drug" and that he might be the "last innocent in rock," it was going to be a stretch for Cocks to attempt to depict a man emerging from formative-years torment. Hints of the darkness that truly shaded Springsteen's story appeared, however, with Springsteen noting, "If I hadn't found music, I don't know what I would have done" or reflecting, "My father never has much to say to me."

Cocks's piece mentioned that Springsteen was "being . . . put down as a product of the Columbia promo 'fog machine' . . ." The *Newsweek* article used what for Cocks was an aside as its central motif. The front cover declaring "Making of a Rock Star" employed a photograph but otherwise was remarkably similar to *Time*'s by showing Springsteen's upper torso while brandishing a guitar and sporting a big grin. The story inside, featuring the same title as the cover strapline, was credited to "Newsweek Staff," who were named in the summary as Maureen Orth, Janet Huck, and Peter S. Greenberg. "Some people are asking whether Bruce Springsteen will be the biggest superstar or the biggest hype of the '70s," the article stated. It quoted Henry Edwards of the *New York Times*: "Springsteen's lyrics are an effusive jumble, his melodies either second-hand or undistinguished, and his performance tedious. Given such flaws there has to be another important ingredient to the success of Bruce Springsteen: namely, vigorous promotion."

Yet like the Cocks and co. article, the feature also admiringly quoted Springsteen's lyrics. It also noted that while DJ Dave Herman had been so disgusted by Columbia's "New Dylan" hype that he didn't bother to listen to his first album, after catching one of his 1975 Bottom Line gigs he publicly apologized for that fact and said on air, "It's the most exciting rock 'n' roll show I've ever seen." *Newsweek* ended on an ambivalent note: "Hypes are as American as Coca-Cola so perhaps—in one way or another—Bruce Springsteen *is* the Real Thing." And perhaps the writers were hedging their bets lest they be proven wrong.

As for Springsteen, he was initially hesitant about signing up to the demands that Appel had made of these two outlets. Not only did he share the opinion of many that *Time* and *Newsweek* were rather un-rock 'n' roll, he also had the feeling of worthlessness that is curiously intertwined in so many celebrities with their bottomless confidence in their own talent and potential. What swung it for him and made him agree to cooperate were the memories of his father, a man who almost always featured in Springsteen songs and stage anecdotes as pathetic. For Springsteen, his dad seemed to spend his life rationalizing his spurning of the opportunities that had come his way, his failure to capitalize on which had left him a bitter man who could obtain pleasure only in such things as mocking his son's musical ambitions. Springsteen may have been accused by some of glamorizing loser figures, but he knew there was nothing "beautiful" about his old man's example of the species and he had no intention of ending up like him.

6 ROADRUNNER: THE TOUR

As Springsteen's popularity grew, his venues . . . didn't. He flat out refused to tour *Born to Run* in halls holding more than three thousand people and spurned television appearances.

The control freak that Springsteen had been in the studio became a somewhat different beast once the sessions had wrapped. Although onstage as passionate as ever, offstage he proved reluctant to promote *Born to Run* on anything other than his own eccentric terms.

For most artists, "touring" an album was a straightforward matter of promoting their latest product to as wide a swath of the culture as possible by being successively present in multiple locales for the purpose of a concert, with the potential for consequent purchases bolstered by the tour's promotional tributaries: radio broadcasts of selected gigs; interviews with periodicals; and assiduous, targeted advertising. Except—as had been obvious from the start—Springsteen was not most artists.

As the tour was being prepared, Springsteen had two stipulations that must have been maddening to Columbia, Appel, and even an arch loyalist like Landau. One was no television appearances. Springsteen's notions about integrity and avoiding selling out at this stage often took convoluted, even nonsensical, forms. The man who might never have become a musician had he not seen an incendiary Elvis performance on the tube inexplicably had something against appearing on the small screen himself. With exposure in that medium becoming as important in the music industry as that on radio waves, it simply meant significant lost sales.

Perhaps there was a subconscious reason for Springsteen originally eschewing venues commensurate with his new fame. After all, when you're at the top, there's only one way to go from there.

(Opposite) His miserable experience in 1973 as support act to the band Chicago in soulless arenas is what put Springsteen off large venues. His viewpoint would change: Within a few years, he would be performing in stadiums—and loving every minute of it.

During a five-night, ten-show residency at the Bottom Line in Greenwich Village, Springsteen's boho outfit is pure rock 'n' roll, but Van Zandt cuts a more sinister figure, one that foreshadows his future *Sopranos* role.

Then there was Springsteen's refusal to perform concerts in any venue holding more than around three thousand people. He had been burned in 1973 by his experience supporting Chicago in arenas. He later said to Paul Williams, "I couldn't play those big places. It has nothing to do with anything that had anything to do with me." This hadn't been much of an issue hitherto, but now that he had acquired wide exposure and was shortly to procure a top-10 album, there were immeasurably more people who wanted to see him in the flesh. Even so, he stuck to this principle even as the *Born to Run* sales mounted.

Another issue was the fact that the album was late to the stores. Springsteen's endless perfectionism and prevarication meant that its release date came more than a full month after the Providence, Rhode Island, gig on July 20 at the Palace Concert Theater that kicked off the tour designed to promote it.

Notwithstanding the theory that gigs whet appetites for product—and certainly no more so than the concerts of a stage meister like Springsteen—it all amounted to a less-than-ideal promotional scenario. In fact, it's difficult not to conclude that—*Born to Run*'s qualities notwithstanding—it's precisely the extravagant publicity that surrounded its release (the type Springsteen so often publicly disdained) that was most responsible for it becoming a *Billboard* #3.

Not that the artist didn't do his bit. Following ten dates at places as varied and out of the way as Lenox, Massachusetts; Kutztown, Pennsylvania; and Akron, Ohio—as well as Washington, D.C.—the tour moved into the Big Apple for a five-night, ten-show residency at the Bottom Line, Greenwich Village. Knowing well the conversion rate of those who caught Springsteen in concert, Columbia made sure to snap up around a quarter of available tickets, some for Columbia staff but many for members of the media.

The tour properly got underway following the Bottom Line gigs. Although Springsteen may not have drawn it up, parts of the itinerary read remarkably like the wish list of an inveterate rocker who knew by heart the lyrics of Bobby Troup's "Route 66" and who wanted to tick off on his bucket list as many of the legendary places from rock 'n' roll history and iconography as possible. The tour comprised Atlanta (three dates); Bryn Mawr, Pennsylvania (presumably lots of female attendees who went on to have great careers in the liberal arts); New Orleans (two dates); Austin, Texas; Houston; Dallas; Oklahoma City (what's the betting that Springsteen declared it "Oh so pretty"?); Grinnell, Iowa; Minneapolis; Ann Arbor, Michigan; Chicago; Iowa City, Iowa; St. Louis; Kansas City, Missouri (what's the betting that the tour bus resounded to an a capella version of the Leiber-Stoller classic?); Omaha, Nebraska; Milwaukee (has made a "beautiful loser" out of me, perhaps?); and Detroit (birthplace of Motown, the Stooges, and Landau's onetime clients, the MC5). On October 10, Springsteen played a hometown gig in New Jersey's Red Bank.

Springsteen is only five foot ten inches tall—something brought into relief when he stood beside Clemons—but his stage charisma gives him the stature of a giant.

THE SUPERSTAR BRACKET: MEETING DYLAN, SPECTOR, AND (ALMOST) ELVIS

"Superstar" was a term that first began to appear during the early 1970s. It would be a stretch to describe Springsteen as a superstar in 1975, but *Born to Run* thrust him into an orbit where he was able to rub shoulders with people who were undoubtedly in that bracket. Some of them were his idols.

Springsteen was introduced to Bob Dylan backstage at a gig on the latter's Rolling Thunder Revue tour, where Dylan told Springsteen, "I hear you're the new me." There was certainly a frisson about the Dylan-Springsteen axis: Rumors circulated that Columbia's Springsteen hype machine was a pointed "screw you" to Dylan for recently abandoning the label for Asylum Records and/or an attempt to fill its departed artist's shoes. Ironically, by the time Springsteen managed to finish *Born to Run*, Dylan was back in the Columbia fold.

Springsteen also got to meet Phil Spector. When Springsteen accepted an invitation to visit a Dion session at the producer's Gold Star Studios in Hollywood fresh from a show at California's Roxy, Spector cracked to his staff—and, like Dylan with his comment, not necessarily meaning anything by it—"Okay, fellas, Bruce Springsteen is here. . . . Let's show him how to make a record." On a more serious note, Spector—naturally cognizant of the fact that Springsteen's new album was in large part a tribute to him—took Springsteen aside and told him that if he were his producer, he would make his records "clearer and better." It was a clear overture for the job, and the idea of a Spector-produced Springsteen album was and is certainly intriguing, but the moment had already passed. Springsteen's agonizing *Born to Run* experience had turned him off to the whole idea of ever again getting involved in big production.

There was the possibility of another encounter with an idol during this period, but this occurred at nobody's invitation and did not result in success. It took part during the "Chicken Scratch" addendum to the *Born to Run* tour that took place early in 1976. Springsteen and band were due to play the Ellis Auditorium in Memphis on April 29. When an inquiry to a local about a good eatery elicited a response that there was a nice joint near Elvis's house, the ears pricked up on the man to whom the King was still so much a hero that he sported an Elvis button on the front of his jacket on *Born to Run*. Once he arrived at Graceland, Springsteen spurned the option of ringing the bell and instead—ever a man-child, in a likable sense—scaled the surrounding stone wall and made his way across its grounds. Nobody responded to his pounding on the front door, but he noticed a patrolling security guard. The two walked toward each other, and Springsteen explained to him he was a fellow musician who would love to meet his hero. It turned out his hero was 2,000 miles away in Lake Tahoe. A disappointed Springsteen told the man his name and asked him to mention him to Elvis when he returned. As his name meant nothing to the security guard, Springsteen was forced into invoking his recent joint appearance on the front of *Time* and *Newsweek*, the promotional supernova about which he had always been so ambivalent.

(Above) Springsteen met Phil Spector in LA after one of his shows at the Roxy in 1975. Spector told the Boss he could make his records "clearer and better."

(Opposite) When Springsteen met Dylan face-to-face during Dylan's Rolling Thunder tour, he told Bruce, "I hear you're the new me."

BRUCE
SPRINGSTEEN
SOLD OUT
THE
ROXY
THEATRE
OCT.
16TH. thru 19TH.
BRUCE SPRINGSTEEN
PERFORMANCE
FRIDAY NITE OCTOBER 17TH at 9:00 P.M.
WILL BE BROADCAST LIVE ON K-WEST 106 F.M.

(Left) The Roxy shows were sold out. Before too long so would Springsteen's arena and stadium shows.

(Below) Columbia Records bought no fewer than half the tickets for the Boss's four-night stint at the Roxy Theatre in West Hollywood. As with the Bottom Line shows, they were trying to spread the word.

The 16th through 19th of that month found the E Street Band on the opposite coast to play four nights at the Roxy Theatre in West Hollywood. This was a similar proposition to the Bottom Line gigs, giving Californians in both the media and the general public the chance to see this new phenomenon and to report back to the world at large. The show was a bit rarified in that this time the label bought *half* the tickets and the audience was peppered with celebrities such as Warren Beatty, George Harrison, Joni Mitchell, and Jack Nicholson. Either way, as at the Bottom Line, the band went down a storm and it unleashed a new wave of Springsteen prominence. (It should not be assumed that Springsteen made an extra effort due to the music media or celebrities in tow: Eyewitness testimony is unanimous that Springsteen will give his all in any concert situation, as evinced by the fact that the following year he played his heart out at a gig in Connecticut at Choate prep school, where he performed for a rumored pittance as a favor to John Hammond, who was a family friend of a student there.)

While national pride to some extent influenced the goodwill toward Springsteen from the American music press, in the UK he had to face journalists with no such patriotic interest in praising him and a general studied skepticism, hence such things as the tenor of the cover of this March 1977 issue of *New Musical Express.*

(Opposite)The four acts advertised as performing at the U.C. Santa Barbara Campus Stadium in October 1976 were at that point pretty much on the same level. Springsteen would ultimately eclipse them all.

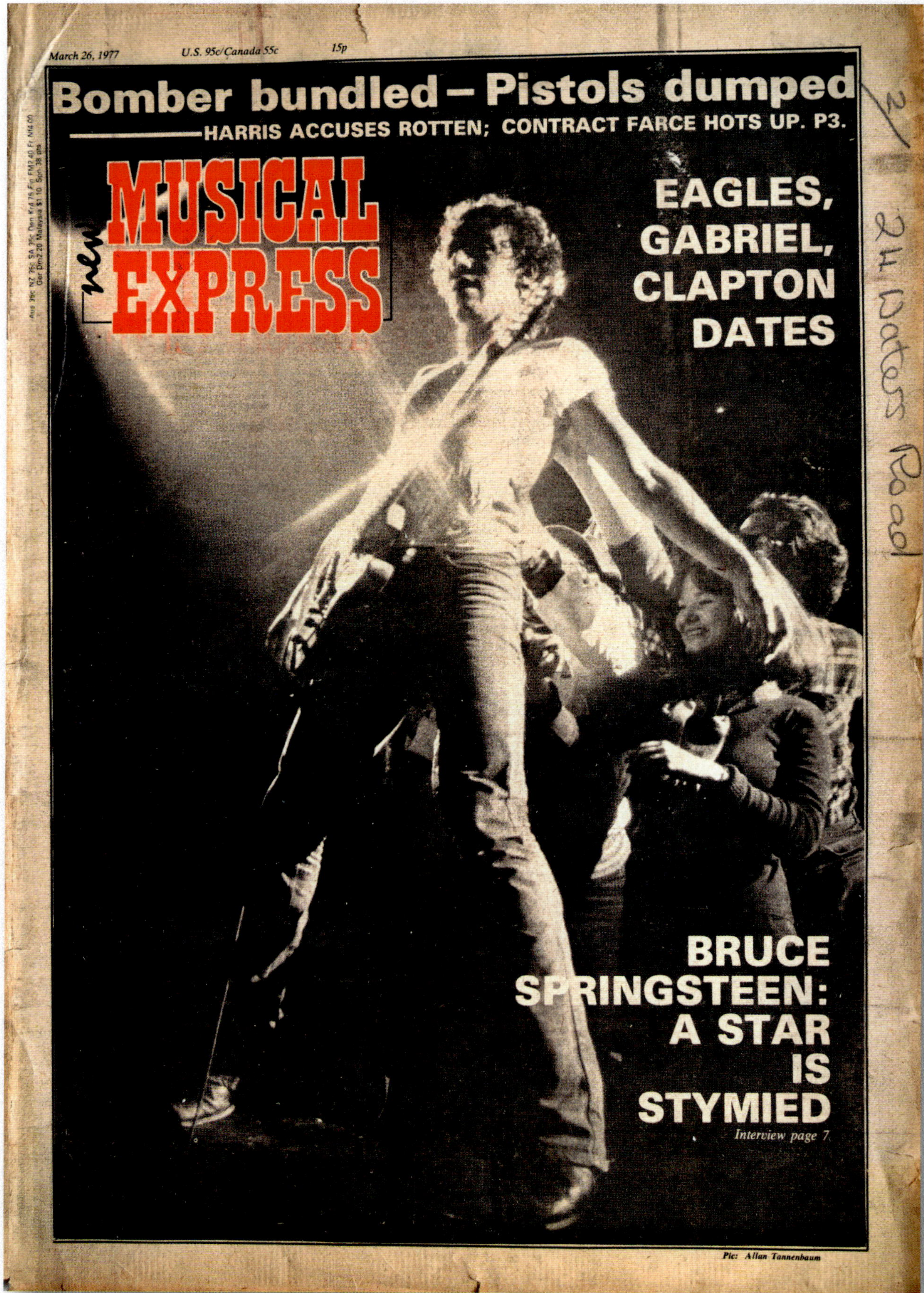

October 23 found Springsteen at New York's Gerde's Folk City, home of some of Bob Dylan's early triumphs. Gigs followed in Portland, Oregon; Seattle; Sacramento, California; Oakland, California; Santa Barbara, California; Tempe, Arizona; Tampa, Florida; and Miami.

There, the first leg of the US tour came to a close. The European leg commenced and closed on November 18 and 24, respectively, at London's Hammersmith Odeon. Sandwiched between were concerts in Sweden and Holland, where, according to Springsteen's biography, the band took in a live sex show in Stockholm and gawked at the women in the windows of Amsterdam's red-light district.

The US tour resumed on December 2 when the E Streeters were really rockin' in Boston. Three dates followed in Washington, D.C. A gig in Pennsylvania's Lewisburg was succeeded on December 11 by another New Jersey homecoming, this one in South Orange, Essex County. A trio of upstate New York appearances (Brookville, Oswego, and Buffalo) was the preamble to the Canadian leg of the tour. From December 19 through 21, the band played in Montreal, Ottawa, and Toronto.

Following a Christmas break, the tour wrapped up with four engagements from December 27 to January 3 at the famed Tower Theater in Upper Darby Township, Pennsylvania.

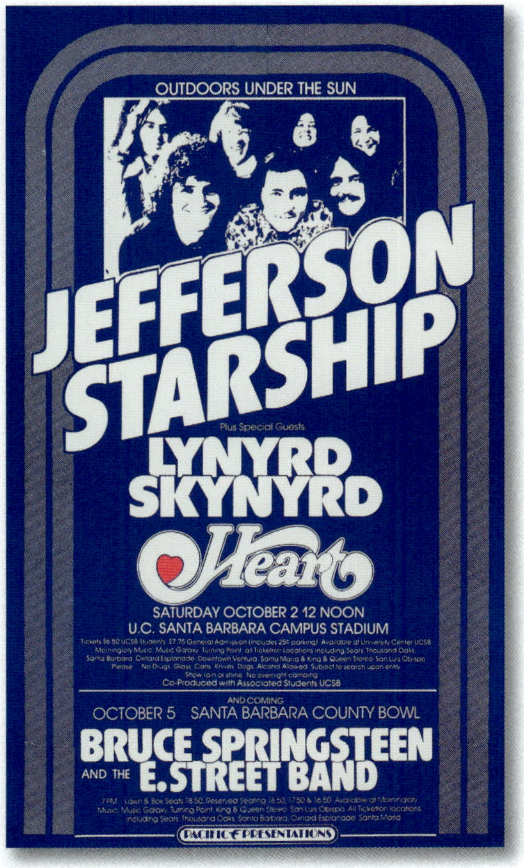

Some people don't consider that to be the end of the tour at all, citing the US jaunt from March 5 to May 28 (the so-called Chicken Scratch tour). Others counter that a resumption of live work after a period of three months hardly fits the idea of touring a record as the term is generally understood, let alone the gigs Springsteen would play from September 1976 to March 1977, which some people also include in the *Born to Run* tour on the grounds that he had yet to release another album.

The explanation for this odd work schedule is that Springsteen was now in a legal dispute with Mike Appel. Springsteen wanted the terms of his original contract with Appel—which he admitted he had signed without reading—to be renegotiated before he would agree to a new deal. When Appel demurred, relations deteriorated. Springsteen sued Appel, Appel countersued, and Springsteen refused to record with either Appel as a producer or anyone Appel nominated. As Springsteen was signed not to Columbia but to Appel's company, it meant a Mexican standoff. On September 15, at the moment of Springsteen's greatest triumph, a judge ruled that Springsteen could not go into a recording studio again until the suits were resolved. Meanwhile, the *Born to Run* monies were frozen, which meant that Springsteen could only keep himself going and his operation afloat by gigging.

The Mike Appel era of the Bruce Springsteen story was over. If *Born to Run* and its success was its main legacy, it was a pretty decent one.

AGGRO AT THE ODEON

The controversy about hype didn't stop at the borders of the United States. On the *Born to Run* tour's European dates, the furor continued and even worsened.

Besides being the last innocent in rock, the Bruce Springsteen of 1975 was a rather parochial individual. He had never left his home state until a trip to California in 1970 when he was past twenty, never driven a car until the same trip, and it wasn't until the *Born to Run* tour when he was in his mid-twenties that he even traveled abroad. However, it wasn't just virgin territory (or the prospect of Continental sex shows) that excited him about the European jaunt.

While Springsteen yielded to no man in his love of indigenous rockers such as Presley and Orbison, Britain was the home of the Beatles, the Rolling Stones, the Animals, the Yardbirds, the Who, Manfred Mann, and all the other fixtures of the tidal wave of British Invasion bands that in the mid-1960s had recast a moribund art form and made it relevant for a new generation, including a young and impressionable Bruce Springsteen. Unfortunately, far from being an ecstatic pilgrimage, the British leg of the jaunt created a distressing scenario that played a part in Springsteen refusing to visit European shores for another half-decade.

Arriving on November 18 at Hammersmith Odeon, the West London venue at which he was booked to play the first of two dates six days apart, he was horrified to find on its backlit marquee the legend, "Finally London Is Ready for Bruce Springsteen and the E Street Band." Inside, he discovered that the foyer and seats were covered with similarly exclamatory posters and flyers. He proceeded to tear posters down in a rage, bawling out Mike Appel as he did so.

Appel has always pleaded innocence. "Nobody asked my permission for that," he told Heylin. Of course, it may be the case that it wouldn't have occurred to the promo people at CBS, UK wing of Columbia, that they should ask such permission. That it was their job to sing the virtues of their artists as loudly as possible is something Springsteen has in subsequent years acknowledged. From the point of view of his twenty-six-year-old self, however, no matter what he did, he could not escape the hype hellhound on his trail. So far in his short career, he'd had to deal with being the New Dylan, Jon Landau's now endlessly quoted "rock-'n'-roll-future"

line, and the *Time* and *Newsweek* double whammy. "I was in this big shadow, man, right from the start," he said that year. "I'm always ten points down, because not only have you got to play, but you got to blow this bullshit out of people's minds first." Springsteen took to the Hammersmith stage a miserable man and left it as one ready to "just drop the whole thing, my career as a musician, because my self-confidence was shot." Not even a second, "by popular demand" date at the Odeon on the 24th could completely salve the psychic wound.

Decades later, he seemed to realize that it might have been all in his head. He sanctioned the release of a DVD and CD of that first Hammersmith Odeon gig, and his accompanying liner notes perhaps unnecessarily proffered the reflective view that he went over better than he recalled. Not having bothered to view the footage for thirty years, he remembered that "the first one was so *bad* I was ready to blow up fuckin' Big Ben." This now seems bewildering—footage of the show reveals it to be slick and passionate, and if he was in a "strop" (as local parlance would put it), none of the appreciative souls in the venue (3,500 to 4,500, according to whom you believe) were able to tell. Even the usually sniffy British music weeklies were by and large impressed.

So what moral can be drawn from this saga? Perhaps only that Bruce Springsteen was a self-absorbed young man, but self-absorbed in a good sense: the sense of somebody who cared that people might think he was so presumptuous as to actually believe what admirers said about him.

(Left) Hype dogged Springsteen's early career. "I'm always ten points down, because not only do you have to play, but you got to blow this bullshit out of people's minds first," he lamented in 1975.

(Above) More imagery from Hammersmith Odeon that suggests Springsteen was better—and happier—than his impressionistic memory suggested.

(Next Spread) Springsteen was convinced that his first gig at London's Hammersmith Odeon was a disaster. Decades later, after finally bringing himself to look at the footage, he realized he was wrong and sanctioned the release of a DVD of it.

7

RIVERS AND RISINGS: THE CAREER

(Left) While the novelty of *Born to Run*'s breakthrough success could never be replicated or relived, there were new worlds to conquer. They would include greater commercial heights, wider critical acclaim, Grammy awards, Academy Awards, a Broadway show, and more.

(Above) While *Born to Run* was infused with intoxicating magic, somber 1978 follow-up *Darkness on the Edge of Town* failed to impress as many people.

Springsteen was prevented from following the commercial breakthrough of *Born to Run* with another album for nearly three years. It was excruciating for both him and his massively expanded army of fans.

Although he continued to write prolifically and to present his new songs to the public at the concerts he continued to play to stay afloat, Springsteen was only able to start the process of building on the breakthrough of *Born to Run* in June 1977 when the case with Appel was resolved. Appel walked away with a reputed $800,000 plus a 2 percent share of the profits of Springsteen's three albums, plus half of the publishing rights of the songs on those records. Springsteen, meanwhile, was now free to be produced and managed by whomever he pleased.

To no one's surprise (least of all a caustic Appel's), Jon Landau became Springsteen's permanent coproducer and manager. To everyone's surprise, *Darkness on the Edge of Town*, the belated follow-up to *Born to Run* that finally appeared in June 1978, had all the loser/proletarian/small town/automobiles-as-escape themes as the preceding album but little of its spiritual or musical uplift. The record's dark and brooding tone was widely imputed to be a consequence of Springsteen's depression about the Appel case. (Elsewhere on the album, Springsteen vented his frustrations with some gut-wrenching

(Left) New album, new look. Beneath the unkempt beard, woolly hats, and scruffy clothes was a rather handsome man.

(Left) A typically jolly stage shot of Springsteen and company. Such scenes mask a more complicated picture involving departures and hiatuses. Still, the E Street Band endures.

guitar work, which now forms the only major remnant of a brief period in the early 1970s when he was, to use his own description, a "big guitar player around town.") The cover of *Darkness* showed Springsteen clean-shaven for the first time since becoming a recording artist. The removal of his beard revealed him to be moodily handsome, something of a revelation for the many who had only ever perceived him as a beanied, slovenly, slightly diminutive quasi-Chaplin.

Those who assumed that the inordinately long gap between *Born to Run* and *Darkness on the Edge of Town* was due only to the lawsuit were proven wrong by the equally inordinate 2⅓-year gap between the latter album and *The River* (1980), an LP where Springsteen was encumbered by no restraints other than his own perfectionism, although it was admittedly a double-set. Unlike during the *Born to Run* sessions, these days the perfectionism took the form not of endless takes and production layering but the discarding of material until he had a collection of songs that precisely fitted his overarching theme.

Some felt Springsteen never equaled *Born to Run*, but others consider the likes of *Darkness on the Edge of Town* and *The River* to exhibit a greater nuance and sophistication in his songwriting.

That theme this time was what happens to a rockin' rebel when the disillusioning realities of life start to make an impression on him. It was winningly adult and vulnerable, epitomized sublimely by "Hungry Heart"'s line, "Don't make no difference what nobody says/Ain't nobody like to be alone." Moreover, on *The River*, Springsteen included all the upbeat styles he had excluded from *Darkness on the Edge of Town*, whether it be pop, up-tempo rock, or frat-rock, while not excluding harrowing downbeat cuts like the title track and "Wreck on the Highway." This and an abandonment of the poetry and myth-making for the vernacular ("Then I got Mary pregnant and, man, that was all she wrote/And for my nineteenth birthday I got a union card and a wedding coat," to quote the exquisite title track) led to a Springsteen album that even the skeptics could love—even if, like almost all two-LP sets, it had a quotient of duds.

The album was Springsteen's first American chart-topper and nudged him even higher in the rock firmament than Born to Run did. His response was completely contrary. In absolute contrast to the thunderous The River, Nebraska (1982) was an extraordinarily spare record. It had been intended to feature the E Street Band, but studio rehearsals convinced Springsteen that vignettes of financial and spiritual poverty like "Reason to Believe" would only work with acoustic guitar and harmonica. Consequently, the demo tape he'd been carrying in his back pocket for several months became his new release. This didn't stop the album from going top 3 on both sides of the Atlantic.

After that hair shirt interregnum came another tilt for all-out commercial dominion, the most intense one yet. Those who thought that by this point Springsteen could get no bigger were proven wrong by *Born in the U.S.A.* (1984). It was a transatlantic chart-topper, went seventeen-times platinum in the United States alone and has to date sold approximately thirty million units worldwide.

REISSUES

When *Born to Run* was first released, there was no such thing as a heritage industry. An album was either in print or—due to declining sales—a cut-out. There was even still a widely held assumption that eventually all albums would one day go out of print as present-day consumers would drift away from such childish concerns as pop music and be supplanted by new generations with younger idols. Perhaps that mentality began to change that very year: 1975 saw the first release of *The Sun Sessions*, a lovingly compiled album that for the first time rounded up all of Elvis Presley's (then) known recordings for his debut label.

As popular music grew into a massive industry staffed not by the type of philistine businessmen who had proliferated in the early days but instead by genuine fans, a reverential, archivist approach began to take hold. It was inevitable that an acknowledged classic such as *Born to Run* would benefit from this.

The *Born to Run* reissues that appeared in 1977 and 1980 were fairly standard, amounting to little more than re-promotions. A 1993 edition was something more substantial: In the age of the compact disc—the format that everyone thought had permanently supplanted vinyl—it was released as a limited-edition gold-colored CD. Some audiophiles declined to be dazzled by the package, pointing out that the contents still sounded better on humble vinyl, but it was still a gratifying mark of respect.

By the time of *Born to Run*'s thirtieth anniversary year, CDs were on their way to obsolescence, their former status as the Future of Music as comical as depictions of twenty-first century life in which silver-suited people routinely soared above cities on their way to work in flying cars. However, fans who continue to cherish the tangibility of handsome artifacts over the convenience of incorporeal downloads were pleased to purchase a celebratory 2005 package containing a CD remaster of the album, a DVD featuring a documentary titled *Wings for Wheels* about its making, and—almost unbelievably after all these years—a film of the fabled first concert at Hammersmith Odeon. Once again, the alleged improvement of the remastered audio element was debatable, but not even a museum could have done a better, more comprehensive job of analyzing and contextualizing the work itself, a scholarly approach that was a measure of just how far popular music had come in the preceding three decades. The package made the *Billboard* top 20.

There was another iteration of *Born to Run* in 2014 as part of the box set *The Album Collection Vol. 1 1973–1984*. The information in the accompanying booklets had some value if one wasn't by now exhausted by the proliferation of remastering jobs.

An image befitting Springsteen's status as one of the last true believers in rock 'n' roll.

The sixteen-month tour of *Born in the U.S.A.* catapulted Springsteen to superstardom. The album was a critically acclaimed hit and its title track—rather than the paean to America some at first assumed—was an unflinching look at recent American history.

For some it's Springsteen's sell-out album. The man who once spurned TV appearances and large venues was now happy to allow his label to mine his new album with utter ruthlessness. Columbia issued no fewer than seven *Born in the U.S.A.* tracks as singles. Releasing more than half an album's contents on 45 rpm had been done before—Michael Jackson's *Thriller* (1982) had also spawned seven 45s—and would be done again, but this was the preserve of artists one could not imagine ever giving a damn about the thought of selling out. Springsteen himself took to the road with a bulked-up body, which he swathed in headbands, neckerchiefs, and quasi-heavy metal outfits. Some found it all beneath him and depressingly symptomatic of a capitulation to corporatism that recently had begun to infect rock.

Even for people who had no problems with such trappings of performance, the album itself felt disturbingly self-parodic, an agglomeration of all the old Springsteen lyrical and musical motifs but not executed as well as before. For others, those were just surface impressions and the album evinced a continued nuance and evolution in Springsteen's art, such as the undermining of the American dream in the title track, the twist ending of "Working on the Highway," the mocking of nostalgia in "Glory Days," and the triumphant embracing of synth-pop with "Dancing in the Dark." Moreover, the up-tempo, tormented "Cover

Bulked up and bandanaed, Springsteen presented a distinct new image on the *Born in the U.S.A.* tour.

Me" and the downbeat, tormented "I'm on Fire" were clearly classics-in-the-making.

For a man hailed by many as the greatest stage performer in rock history, a live-in-concert album was always in the cards. When it came in 1986, Springsteen opted not for the traditional route of a facsimile of a single concert but instead for a career overview. *Live 1975–1985* (the first Springsteen album on which the E Street Band was featured in the artist credit) was appropriate for an artist prone to perform three-hour shows—a marathon listening experience. It took a five-LP set to house it (later three CDs). As a documentary of live Springsteen, it was all here, from his relatively ramshackle performances at the Roxy in 1975 to his wowing of the multitudes at Giants Stadium ten years later with a show both supremely slick and somewhat choreographed. Springsteen's rambling reminiscences of childhood—often mid-song—were left intact to give a genuine flavor of what it's like to see him in the flesh. The participatory party atmosphere of a Springsteen gig was also in evidence, the quintessence of which is shown in the way that Springsteen doesn't even need to sing the first verse of "Hungry Heart" in a 1980 rendition at the Nassau Coliseum, New York.

A similar long-anticipated extravaganza of a release was *Tracks* (1998). Aside from Bob Dylan, never has an artist discarded perfectly good songs the way Bruce Springsteen has. Like Dylan, the Boss has

THE BOSS
HOBOKEN

(Left) Steve Van Zandt's replacement Nils Lofgren provides a moment of levity during one of the Boss's habitually exhausting stage performances.

seemed to take an almost perverse pleasure in abandoning completed masters that often rank with his very best recordings. He wrote more than fifty tracks each for *Darkness on the Edge of Town*, *The River*, and *Born in the U.S.A.,* and immediately consigned the bulk of them to the vaults. By the turn of the millennium, he had not released the vast majority of songs he had recorded. Also like Dylan, this inclination for what others see as wastefulness has caused frustration among fans, an angst that bootleggers have been more than happy upon which to capitalize. As with Dylan with his *Bootleg Series* of archive releases, Springsteen relented and began issuing his abandoned material, starting with *Tracks*. A four-CD set, its track listing alone is breathtaking stuff: sixty-six songs, constituting more than four hours' worth of material, enough to fill six albums at old vinyl standards. That is remarkable enough in itself—his discards would constitute the bulk of a career for another artist—but what is even more remarkable is the stunning quality of much of this material, whether it be the searing, anti-nuclear power *River* outtake "Roulette" or buffed-up 1973 discard "Thundercrack." As mentioned, *Born to Run* is an outlier in his canon in having few outtakes. The weaker songs on the set include its two *Born to Run* outtakes, "Linda Let Me Be the One" and "So Young and in Love."

Some long-term Springsteen fans disdained *Born in the U.S.A.* as self-parody, but it went platinum seventeen times over and moved thrity million units worldwide.

In 2010 came *The Promise*, comprising outtakes from the *Darkness* sessions, including at last his version of "Because the Night," which he had donated to the Patti Smith Group in 1978 and had seen them have a transatlantic hit with it. *The Ties That Bind: The River Collection* was released in 2015 and included an alternate version of Springsteen's fifth album and twenty-two additional outtakes that amounted to an old vinyl double-LP.

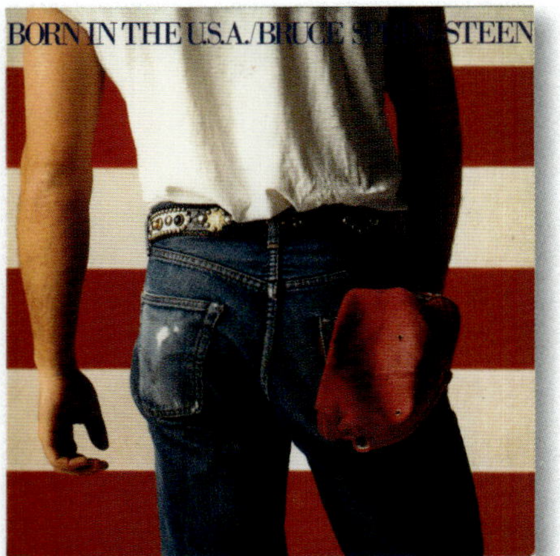

Meanwhile, in 2014, Springsteen embarked on a campaign of official internet concert releases from across his career. By 2024, there were over a hundred of them. People who once fantasized about more Springsteen were now drowning in him.

BORN TO RUN CONCERTS

Once upon a time, Bruce Springsteen played a selection of tracks from *Born to Run* during concerts that also featured songs from the other albums in his small canon. For a brief period in the mid-1970s, the *Born to Run* songs were the centerpiece of his gigs. As his canon grew, the *Born to Run* songs occupied an increasingly smaller proportion of his setlist. While the album never lost its allure and status—most Springsteen fans continue to nominate it as their favorite Springsteen effort—there came a startling point in the early 1980s where he made its title track an opening song. An artist has truly achieved immortality when he can toss off an iconic recording like "Born to Run" as a curtain raiser. Even now, it's not a live centerpiece but an encore number.

The wheel turned again when the *Born to Run* album became, at least occasionally, the be-all and end-all of his concerts. In the twenty-first century, artists began acquiescing to a demand for performances in which an album wasn't represented by selected tracks but rather played in its entirety from start to finish. Springsteen first went this route in 2008 at New Jersey's Count Basie Theater when performing a benefit for the Red Bank venue. (It being the case that a man known for three-hour concerts could hardly proffer a set of forty minutes duration, he and the E Streeters also did *Darkness on the Edge of Town*.) The exercise has been repeated several times since. The following year, the autumn 2009 leg of the *Working on a Dream* tour saw them do it repeatedly, as did the 2013 *Wrecking Ball* world tour.

Some will always be dubious about the entire concept: Rare are the albums on which every track is great, so why bother with a performance that inevitably ebbs when it gets to a work's lesser cuts? Others love the whole notion of a live replication of the aural experience they've known for so many years, with all the familiar warps and wefts. As Patti Scialfa noted, "When you hear them in order, it brings you back to the first time you heard them as a listener."

A peculiar adjunct to this story is that in 2024, Springsteen decided to start some concerts with "So Young and in Love," that utterly unremarkable and uncharacteristic *Born to Run* outtake.

(Left) Though Patti Scialfa, Max Weinberg, Steve Van Zandt, and the Boss have gray hairs and are thicker around the middle, they still fill stadiums.

(Opposite) Just a few years before Clemons's 2011 death, the "Big Man" and the Boss perform at a concert in San Jose.

HEARTLAND ROCK

It's often been said that while he may have made much great art, Bruce Springsteen has never proffered anything more novel than a synthesis of all the music upon which he was raised. This is debatable: as discussed previously, he is surely the main originator of class-based popular music. In addition to that, though, is the fact that he significantly boosted and altered the development of an entire genre: the blue-collar, fist-pumping style that came to be known as heartland rock.

It is essentially a type of music that is noticeably—if sometimes only implicitly—

more working class than most rock. Not necessarily political, but big on the communitarianism of proletarian communities where shared experience of hardship create much in the way of emotional solidarity. Musically, the genre is classic rock crossed with Americana and roots, with an emphasis on anthemic melody.

Springsteen can't really be said to have invented it, because artists who preceded him such as Bob Seger and peers such as Southside Johnny and the Asbury Jukes fit the mold perfectly. At least some lineage can be traced to artists as far back as Hank Williams, Woody Guthrie, and Creedence Clearwater Revival. What Springsteen did—particularly from *Born to Run* onward—is to provide a solid artistic template and a commercial market for this type of music. Without him, it's impossible to imagine the careers of so many other artists considered to be heartland, among them Tom Petty, John Cougar/Mellencamp, Bruce Hornsby & the Range, Lucinda Williams, and even Bon Jovi.

(Left) Toward the end of his 1975 live commitments, Springsteen had the pleasure of performing a homecoming gig at Seton Hall University, in Essex County, New Jersey.

Tunnel of Love (1987) was the first Springsteen album to feature Van Zandt's replacement Nils Lofgren, a singer-songwriter of vast talents and an often impressive solo career himself. It was a surprisingly depressive work considering that it appeared only a couple of years after Springsteen's marriage to model Julianne Phillips. The reason why became apparent when Phillips filed for divorce in 1988, citing as grounds Springsteen's relationship with backing singer Patti Scialfa. In retrospect, the doubts and uncertainty in tracks like "Brilliant Disguise" indicated a man who entered marriage too hastily. The lyrics explore personal rather than sociological issues while musically the album has a very spartan feel—Springsteen often spurning the E Street Band for machinery—as though Springsteen was trying to make the music reflect his spiritual desolation.

Releasing two albums on the same day, as Springsteen did in 1992 with *Human Touch* and *Lucky Town*, was hardly in keeping with his oft-stated sympathy for the working man: A double album would have cost his fans less money. There were mutterings about how Springsteen might have forgotten his roots during his recent relocation from his New Jersey hometown to a mansion in Hollywood. The supposition was that he wanted to break into movies. He succeeded on one level with "Streets of Philadelphia," his 1994 Oscar-winning theme song from the movie *Philadelphia* and his Academy Award–nominated 1996 title tune to *Dead Man Walking*.

He'd certainly left his musical roots behind. Except for keyboardist Roy Bittan, the E Street Band were now gone. The musicians with which Springsteen replaced them on *Human Touch* were vastly inferior, particularly Jeff Porcaro, whose teeth-grating, click-tracked drumming was simply not in the same league as the skins work of Max

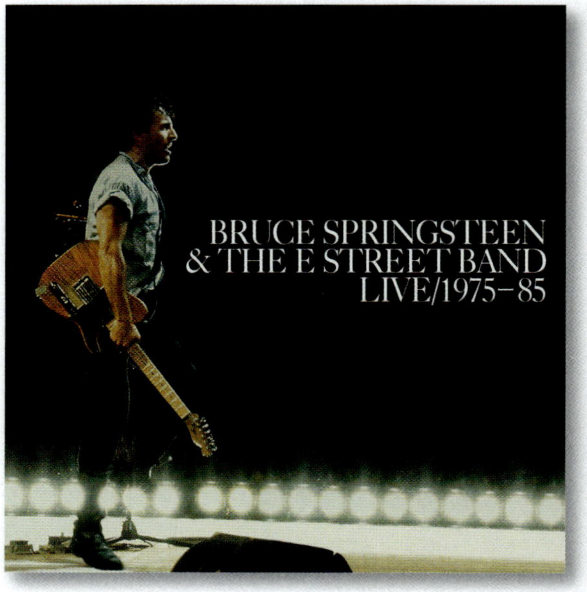

Nils Lofgren had an impressive career before he even joined the E Street Band, fronting cult powerhouse trio Grin and releasing several solo albums. Here, he performs in Europe in July 1987.

Weinberg. The songs were generally love numbers, although Springsteen's perennial thoughtfulness as a writer made them a cut above mere genre pop.

Human Touch had been mostly recorded in 1990, but Springsteen delayed its release because he felt it needed another track. When he returned to the studio, he ended up with enough songs to fill a further album, one that, because it addressed more serious concerns than the previously recorded material, he felt should be consumed as a separate entity. On *Lucky Town,* Springsteen plays everything except drums. This coupled with rather vague melodies and mumbled singing make for a somewhat insubstantial sound. Yet the lyrics frequently jolt the listener upright at their excellence ("It's a sad man, my friend, who's living in his own skin and can't stand the company").

Human Touch and *Lucky Town* marked a turning point: No one was claiming that they were classic or even great albums, nor really would anyone make such a claim for any future Springsteen work, even despite him hooking up with the E Street Band again in 1999. He had contracted the same syndrome that had afflicted his own idols: His musical technique and personal wisdom were by definition more acute than ever, but, rather than this translating into greater art, it preceded a diminution of quality. The explanation for this apparent conundrum is that once having proven artistic worth, the hunger to continue doing so becomes less intense. Meanwhile, new priorities in life emerge, such as being a spouse and parent (Springsteen and his second wife, Scialfa, have three children). Just as had happened with the Stones, Dylan, the solo Beatles, et al., Springsteen's continued success would be predicated on what he had accomplished in the past; he remains a huge concert draw, but with few calls from the stalls for tracks from his new album.

And yet . . . it's not quite as simple as that. For depressing as a protracted decline may be, with Springsteen it never incurs contempt in long-term fans like the longueurs of the careers of McCartney, the Stones, and Dylan have done. His perennial thoughtfulness and integrity have resulted in an extraordinary level of goodwill being extended to him.

There again, it's precisely because of that man-of-the-people image that he will forever endure a scrutiny that others escape. Witness the furor surrounding his first compilation, *Greatest Hits* (1995). The chief complaint amongst Springsteen followers was its four previously unreleased tracks: Surely Springsteen was precisely not the type of artist who would make long-term followers pay for songs they already owned to acquire novelties and rarities? Or the controversy over the way he crossed a picket line on the way to a gig in October 1992. Or the fact that he has charged eye-popping prices for concert

The late 1980s and early 1990s were tough for Springsteen. For one reason or another, Van Zandt, Springsteen's first wife Julianne Phillips, and the E Street Band all ceased to be part of his life. He found happiness, though, with singer Patti Scialfa, who became his life partner and mother to his three children. He and the E Street Band would reunite.

tickets long past the point where he has amassed more wealth than he can ever spend in several lifetimes.

However, which major star other than Springsteen would make an album like *The Ghost of Tom Joad* (1995)? On an album that could almost be called *Nebraska II*, he once again tackles big themes with small music, guitar and harmonica often his only companions as he takes the listener through the dust bowls and flophouses traversed by the poor, the itinerant, and the unloved. Who but Springsteen would record *We Shall Overcome: The Seeger Sessions*, a collection of thirteen traditional tunes popularized by Pete Seeger, a man whose political activism and songwriting was in the McCarthyite era literally a danger to his livelihood? Who but Springsteen would write "American Skin (41 Shots)," a song about a man whose body was riddled with bullets by New York police? Then there is the simple, utterly moving fact that at every concert he miraculously sings every song with a joy and an enthusiasm that suggests it's not for the ten-thousandth time but the very first.

Does Springsteen write so obsessively about the underprivileged because he feels guilty about his wealth? Is he trying in his songs to preserve in amber the dirt-poor, troubled young man he long ago ceased to be—and making money in that peculiar, convoluted process? Does it matter? As far as is humanly possible for a man who will never go hungry again, he has remained wedded to his humanitarian values and working-class roots, the ones he so acutely laid out in *Born to Run*. It would be churlish to ask for more.

PHOTO CREDITS

Alamy Stock Photos: 6, White House Photo; 8l, ARCHIVIO GBB; 8r, ARCHIVIO GBB; 12, Tom Hill, WireImage; 15l, ARCHIVIO GBB; 18, Pictorial Press; 21r, Bill Waterson; 25, Yuriy T; 31, Bill Waterson; 39, Edward Roth; 40, Tim Merrick; 42, ZUMA; 51b, Richard Levine; 75, John Ares; 92, Pictorial Press; 93, Gijsbert Hanekroot; 94, kpa; 100tl, SilverScreen; 100, tr; JT Vintage; 100b, Nina Reistad; 107, John Ares; 125, Gijsbert Hanekroot; 127r, Bill Waterson; 140, Some Wonderful Old Things; 141, Bill Waterson; 162, John Ares.

Associated Press: 15, 16, SIPPL SIPA PRESS; 23.

John. T Comerford | Frank White Photo Agency: Frontis; 104.

Getty Images: 4, Tom Hill, WireImage; 20l, The Estate of David Gahr; 20r, Michael Ochs Archives; 21l, Allan Tannenbaum; 22, Lynn Goldsmith, Corbis Premium Historical; 27, The Estate of David Gahr; 26, MediaNews Group/Reading Eagle; 28, The Estate of David Gahr; 30, Gary Gershoff; 33, Kevin Kane, WireImage; 34, Tom Hill, WireImage; 35, Michael Ochs Archives; 36, Allan Tannenbaum; 37l, M. McKeown, Hulton Archive; 37r, Michael Ochs Archives; 38, Nicholas Hunt; 43, Michael Ochs Archives; 44, Michael Ochs Archives; 45, The Estate of David Gahr; 46, Erica Echenberg, RedFerns; 48, The Estate of David Gahr; 50, Amy Sussman; 52, Tom Hill, WireImage; 53r, Kevin Mazur; 54, Allan Tannenbaum; 56, Richard E. Aarons, RedFerns; 58, The Estate of David Gahr; 60, Nicholas Russell; 62, Allan Tannenbaum; 64, Richard E. Aarons, RedFerns; 65, LMPC; 66, Tim Mosenfelder, Hulton Archive; 67t, IFA Film; 67b, Michael Ochs Archives; 68, Fin Costello, RedFerns; 70, Gary Gershoff; 72, Allan Tannenbaum; 73, Dick Darrell, Toronto Star; 74, Richard E. Aaron, Redferns; 76 Clayton Call, Redferns; 78, Rob Verhorst/RedFerns; 80, Allan Tannenbaum; 82, Fin Costello, Redferns; 84, Fin Costello, Redferns; 86, Tom Hill, WireImage; 87, Tom Hill, Michael Ochs Archives; 88, Richard E. Aaron, Redferns; 89, Michael Ochs Archives; 90, Tom Hill, WireImage; 95, Frans Schellekens, RedFerns; 96, Allan Tannenbaum; 98, Fin Costello, RedFerns; 102, Merry Alpern, Corbis Historical; 106, Fin Costello, RedFerns; 108, Tom Hill, WireImage; 109, LMPC; 110, Tom Hill, WireImage; 111l, Janet Fries, Archive Photos; 111r, LMPC; 112, Tom Hill, WireImage; 113, Ebet Roberts, Redferns; 114, Tom Hill, WireImage; 116t, Michael Putland, Hulton Archive; 116b, Andrew Putler, Redferns; 117, Roberta Bayley, Redferns; 118, Nobby Clark/Popperfoto; 119, Fin Costello, Redferns; 120, Fin Costello, Redferns; 124, American Stock; 127l, Gijsbert Hanekroot; 128, Lynn Goldsmith, Corbis Historical; 130, Michael Ochs Archives; 131, Tom Hill, Michael Ochs Archives; 132, The Estate of David Gahr; 134, The Estate of David Gahr; 136, Frank Edwards; 137, David Redfern, Redferns; 138, Fotos International; 139, Michael Ochs Archives; 142, Michael Putland, Hulton Archive; 143, Gus Stewart, Redferns; 144, Brooks Kraft, Sygma; 145, Koh Hasebe/Shinko Music, Hulton Archive; 146, Aaron Rapoport, Corbis Historical; 147, San Francisco Chronicle/Hearst Newspapers; 148, Mark Weiss, WireImage; 150, Rick Diamond; 153, Clayton Call, Redferns; 156, Michael Putland, Hulton Archive; 154, David Tan/Shinko Music, Hulton Archive; 156, Aaron Rapoport, Corbis Historical; 157, Richard McCaffrey, Michael Ochs Archive; 158, Aaron Rapoport, Corbis Historical; 159, Chris Walter, WireImage; 160, Mario Skraban, Redferns; 161, Rocky M. Widener, FilmMagic; 164, Frans Schellekens, Redferns; 166, Gary Gershoff.

Photofest: 24.

Quarto Publishing Group Collection: 9, 14, 32, 123, 126l, 126r, 149, 159, 163l, 163r.

Shutterstock: 85.

Laurens Van Houten | Frank White Photo Agency: 10.

INDEX

SPRINGSTEEN
THE ROXY–OCT. 16-19
Born to Run
"BORN TO RUN." THE NEW ALBUM FROM BRUCE SPRINGSTEEN.
ON COLUMBIA RECORDS AND TAPES.